Chinese Dia
for the King *of* Kings
BY
ROSALIND GOFORTH

"God hath made of one Blood all Men under Heaven."

FOREWORD

Whole libraries have been written on Christian evidences. The resources of philosophic and scientific research have been drawn up in defence of the Christian faith. Yet important as these are, it may be questioned whether any or all of them together bring home to the heart such conviction as does the story of a redeemed soul—a soul lifted out of the fearful pit and miry clay—cleansed, purified and established in righteousness. Whatever intellectual difficulties may occur, a countenance illumined with a light that is not of this world is irresistible.

Henry Ward Beecher spoke of a nest of infidels he had encountered upon whom argument made little impression. There lived in the same village a humble washerwoman of singularly beautiful character. When asked what they thought of her the sceptics were silenced. Harold Begbie says of Old Born Drunk that "he advertised salvation. Before the miracle of Old Born Drunk the arguments of the tavern atheist melted into thin air."

We are indebted to Mrs. Goforth for having gathered from her long experience in China a series of instances as convincing as any told by Harold Begbie in "Twice Born Men." They are not the outcome of generations of development, for China has no religious background. They are miracles of grace. Luther said, "God is the God of the humble, the miserable, the oppressed, the desperate, of them that are naught. It is His nature to give sight to the blind, to comfort the broken hearted and to justify the ungodly."

The divine nature is beautifully and impressively illustrated by these stories of redeemed and glorified ones whose after life verified the reality of the miraculous change. He is able to save unto the uttermost. With Him there is plenteous redemption. Go ye, therefore, and tell it out.

(REV.) R. P. MACKAY, D.D.

INTRODUCTION

The following sketches are as photographically true as my knowledge of Chinese life and people can make them. They are written primarily as an answer to the oft met questions, "Do missions pay?" and, "After all, are there any real Christians in China?"

We missionaries are frequently told that the average church member at home has come to think of missionaries' letters as "too dry to read."

Wherefore, my attempt to give missionary facts in a different, possibly more readable, form. With what success remains to be seen. The little book is sent forth with the earnest hope and prayer that those who read these sketches may come to see the truth of what Paul said: "God hath made of ONE BLOOD all men under heaven."

ROSALIND GOFORTH.

Kikungshan, South Honan, China,

July 24, 1920.

SKETCH I

As Silver Is Refined

PART 1: THE BIRTH OF A SOUL.
PART 2: FROM GLEAM TO GLORY.

As Silver Is Refined

Part I. THE BIRTH OF A SOUL.

One sultry afternoon in June, 19—, an elderly woman. seated in the shade of her front gateway, the coolest spot she could find, was fanning vigorously in vain attempt to keep cool, discontented mutterings keeping time to her fan. It was time the long summer siesta ended and for folks to get to work, so thought Mrs. Dwan, but "folks" evidently thought otherwise, for the whole village seemed as still and lifeless as a graveyard.

Just as the woman was about to rouse the sleeping household her attention was attracted to a man wheeling a barrow on which lay a sick child. Putting his barrow down opposite the Dwan's gateway the man wiped his steaming brows as he stepped forward saying, "Honorable Lady, my child is very thirsty, we have come a long way, will you give us water?"

"Gladly," said the woman, hastening into the inner court as fast as her excessive avoirdupois would permit. In a moment or two she reappeared, not with ice cold water as in our country, but with a kettle of boiling water and two bowls.

"Wheel the child into the shade and rest yourself," said the woman as she filled the bowls; then setting one down beside the sick child, she motioned to the man to take a seat on the stone steps. "Where are you going," she

4

asked by way of opening the conversation.

"I'm taking my child to the foreign doctor at W———."

"What!" she exclaimed, with a look of horror, "you are surely never going to venture inside that place! We have heard some terrible things about those people."

"Well," replied the man, "all I can say is this, a neighbor woman of ours went to that hospital perfectly blind and came back seeing almost as well as you or I. A man in my village had a terrible leg, he would certainly have died, but he went there too and came back healed. He told us the doctor treated him as well as the patients who could pay, though they knew he was too poor to pay."

"But, why then do people talk so?" persisted Mrs. Dwan.

"You know the proverb," replied the man, with rather a contemptuous shrug, "You can bridle a horse or a mule, but who can bridle a woman's tongue." With this parting thrust and a polite bow, the man caught up his barrow and hurried on.

Mrs. Dwan's husband was what is known in China as the "leading man" of his region. He was a landowner of considerable means, and was widely known and sought after as a doctor though he had no knowledge whatever of Western methods of treating diseases, nor of surgery, but was an expert in the art of "needle pricking," a common Chinese treatment not infrequently used with fatal results.

As the man with the barrow disappeared in the distance, Dr. Dwan appeared at his dispensary gateway, across the street from where his wife was sitting. Calling him to her she related what had just passed. The Doctor listened, but said nothing; paying no attention to the fierce denunciation of the missionaries with which she ended; her husband had learnt through many years of bitter experience with her to say little but act. When the following morning the Doctor announced his intention of taking the younger son to the foreign Doctor to have a growth on his foot removed, of course, Mrs. Dwan began to storm and rage but to no purpose, except to give matter of interest to her neighbors, trouble to her household, and sickness to herself. Her fits of temper were so violent and sustained that it is little wonder Nature usually had her way by a general collapse, when the naturally strong woman would lie for days as helpless as a child.

5

As Dr. Dwan started off for the Mission Hospital, it would be too much to imagine that his mind was quite free from fear or doubt, but his intense curiosity to see the foreign Doctor about whom he had heard such conflicting reports, and a desire, if possible, to see something of his methods of treatment, overcame every other thought. A walk of some twelve English miles brought them to the city of W———. On reaching the Mission Hospital they found themselves in the midst of a crowd of sick and suffering ones. Procuring their tickets of admission they joined themselves to the queue moving towards the Dispensary door. The moment Dr. Dwan found himself and his child, with a dozen or more others, ushered into the Doctor's presence, all fears vanished,—who, indeed, could not trust those keen, quiet, kind eyes?

Stepping aside purposely so that the others might be treated first and thus give him his chance to watch the foreigner, Dr. Dwan made the most of his opportunity. At last the assistant called him forward to take his name. The moment he had given it, Dr. Blank, the missionary, looked up quickly and said, "Why, are you Dr. Dwan of C———?"

"That is my unworthy name," replied the other. Immediately Dr. Blank left the patient he was treating, and came forward with such a friendly smile the Chinese doctor was completely taken by surprise.

"I'm very pleased indeed to meet you," the missionary said heartily, and in a few moments had the other quite at his ease. From their first meeting these two men drew naturally together. The missionary doctor recognized in Dr. Dwan the true instincts of a physician and generously remembered that this man's ignorance and inefficiency as a doctor was not due to lack of natural ability but from the lack of advantages such as he himself had enjoyed.

The removal of the growth on the boy's foot was a simple operation, but it required the administration of chloroform. When this was about to be given the father showed decided nervousness, but a few quiet firm words from Dr. Blank allayed his fears. He stood aside and watched with intense wonder and admiration every detail of the operation.

Dr. Blank saw the man's keen interest in everything connected with the Hospital, and arranged for the care of his boy so that the father could be with him in the operating room, the afternoon clinic, and ward visitation. When the work of the day was over the missionary sometimes invited Dr. Dwan to his study in his house at the rear of the compound. It was at such times the missionary doctor opened to his less favored brother the way of Salvation.

It was not till the close of his stay that Dr. Dwan seemed to really understand. The two men were talking in the study when Dr. Dwan spoke out suddenly as if to get something off his mind:

"Dr. Blank, I have a request I find hard to make."

Dr. Blank's face fell as visions of many past requests came before him, but he said merely:

"What can I do for you?"

"The fact is," continued the other, "people say you have strange things in your home. Would you allow me to see the place?"

The missionary jumped to his feet with a relieved smile saying, "Why, come along now. I'll show you everything." Through the house they went; each room seemed more wonderful to Dr. Dwan than the last, everything was a wonder, but what especially aroused his admiration and astonishment was the school-room where the missionaries' children—girls as well as boys—were at their lessons. All he saw made a deeper impression on his mind than the missionary or even he himself at the time realized.

Some days later when in conversation with one of the missionaries something like the following took place:

Dr. Dwan, looking intently at the missionary, suddenly said with deep feeling, "Do you know what people are saying about you all?"

"Yes, I think we do," returned the other, with a little laugh. "At least we know quite enough."

"Then I cannot understand how you can stay and do what you are doing with my people."

"My friend," replied the missionary, drawing his chair nearer to the other and speaking from the depths of a full heart, "It is like this, Jesus Christ left His home in heaven to suffer and die for us—for me. The love that made Him do that He has given to me and those with me. It is this LOVE that makes us do all this for your people."

"You mean then that you are just following in Jesus Christ's steps—just doing as He did?"

"Yes," came the answer quietly, "just that. Will you follow Him too?"

7

There was a firm and set purpose in Dr. Dwan's face as, after a moment's pause, he said gravely:

"Yes, I will, I will follow the Lord Jesus."

* * *

This man counted not the cost; he simply saw the Gleam and faced for it. Little did he dream how short and stormy the path would be that led from the Gleam to the Glory beyond.

Part II. FROM GLEAM TO GLORY.

> "The Son of God goes forth to war
> A kingly crown to gain;
> His blood-red banner streams afar:
> Who follows in His train?
> Who best can drink his cup of woe,
> Triumphant over pain,
> Who patient bears his cross below—
> He follows in His train."

When Dr. Dwan informed his family that he had become a Christian, or as they put it, "become a slave of the foreigners," it was as if a thunder-bolt had fallen in their midst.

The first step the doctor felt he must take as master of his own home, was to destroy the household gods. While the first ones were being torn down, the family were too terror-stricken to offer any resistance, but by the time the "kitchen god" was reached Mrs. Dwan had somewhat recovered her senses and stood before the stove over which the god was pasted, prepared to fight.

Firmly, without undue violence, her husband put her aside, and, securing the god crumpled all together in his hands, (for they were made of paper), he faced the crowd which filled the court; here, for almost an hour the brave man preached with intense earnestness of the love of the One True God in giving His Son for them. He then kindled the gods and burnt them before the crowd, who, when all was over, dispersed, but with black looks and ominously quiet.

For many months Dr. Dwan labored among his neighbors and through the whole region trying to win men to his new faith, but public opinion was too strongly against him. It was universally believed,—by his family as well as outsiders—that the foreigners had bewitched him and that the gods would certainly wreak their vengeance upon him. Strange to say, what followed, tended to strengthen them in this belief.

A railway, which had recently been built by foreigners, passed over part of Dr. Dwan's land. One day, soon after he had come out as a Christian, one of the doctor's hired men was ploughing a piece of this land with a yoke of oxen (or mules). When crossing the rails, and blinded by a dust-storm which was blowing, the man did not notice the train which struck and killed both animals, though the heathen hired man remained uninjured.

The most precious possession a man can have in China, next to a son, is a grandson. Dr. Dwan had one such treasure; a fine healthy child, he was the pride and joy of both grandparents. Soon after the above accident had come to try the new Christian's faith, this child took ill suddenly and died. We can only imagine what a tremendous test this must have been to the grandfather's faith.

Shortly after the grandchild's death the eldest son purchased an animal at a fair; after it had been put with the other animals it was discovered to have a distemper, and, though at once removed the mischief was done, for a few days later most of the doctor's animals were dead. They were indeed dark days, and through all these special testings which I have mentioned, was the unceasing nagging and at times violent raging of his wife; but later the testimony was given that through it all Dr. Dwan's faith in God never flinched.

When feeling the need of help and encouragement, a visit to his friend the foreign doctor, never failed to give fresh courage. But darker days were in store for him, and he surely needed all the help his fellow Christian could give.

One day a deputation waited upon him to ask for his contribution towards the village theatrical held in honor of the village god. Dr. Dwan received them courteously, and endeavored to show them how impossible it was for him to give to such an object now that he worshipped the One Only and True God. When finally the deputation saw that they could not move him, they left in anger, threatening, that since he chose to go against the will of the people, he must take the consequences. The price he had to pay for this stand we shall see.

A few days after the above took place, the doctor's watchdogs were both found poisoned. The Chinese depend very much upon these dogs for

9

protection against thieves, who are everywhere in this land. From this on the neighbors carried on a system of petty thieving of the doctor's property which continued till within a short time of his death. The village people, as is general in China, worked their farms on the co-operative plan, at least to the extent of sharing as common property many necessary farming implements. When Dr. Dwan came to require these as was his right, they were refused. Patients ceased to come, and calls from a distance became a thing of the past. In a hundred ways he was subject to petty persecution. When these failed to "bring him to his senses," more serious action was planned.

One day when the doctor was away from home, the news reached him that his barn and dispensary had been set on fire and burned. A few months later, just before the wheat harvest, his wheat field was set on fire. And through it all he stood alone with his God,—never shrinking, never doubting.

Then, as if God saw he needed but the final refining, malignant cancer of the throat brought his body low. It was then that the tide of Public Opinion seemed to turn. His wife even began to show signs of real change. She no longer opposed her husband, but it was not till much later that she seemed to be really converted. The eldest son, who had all along been secretly with his father, now came out boldly as a Christian; and from the time when Dr. Blank gave his verdict that Dr. Dwan could not live, he devoted himself to his father endeavoring in every possible way to make up for the past. Even his heathen neighbors began to ask themselves, "Have we done this man wrong?"

The missionaries from W—— made frequent visits to the dying Christian, and as every detail of these visits was discussed by all the villagers (everything is done openly in this land) there is little doubt but that the love and interest shown by the foreigners on these visits had much to do with the rapidly changed attitude towards Christianity.

Before Dr. Dwan passed away, he had the joy of hearing that his two sons, his elder son's wife, as well as several of his neighbors had become Christians.

As this saint's last struggle ended and his last breath was drawn, we can almost hear the welcome that awaited him, and the Saviour's voice as He said,—"Well done good and faithful servant—enter thou into the joy of thy Lord."

* * *

Within three years of Dr. Dwan's death, the writer witnessed the destruction of the village Temple.—destroyed by PUBLIC CONSENT that the materials might be used in building a Christian Church on the outskirts of the village, the land on which the Church was built being given by one of the men who so bitterly persecuted the first Christian.

It was in this little village Church the writer heard some of the finest personal testimonies she has ever heard. It was the last of a week's special meetings, the leader had given opportunity for any who wished to give a personal testimony; in an instant a poor working man was on his feet, as if afraid lest others would get ahead of him. This is what he said:

"Please, Pastor, I want to tell how I know God answers prayer. I was wheeling a barrow full of coal down a steep place the other evening when it broke down. I did not dare leave my barrow or the coal would be stolen, and I did not dare stay there or I would freeze, so I just knelt down by the roadside and asked God to send some one to help me. As I was praying a man came along, and seeing me on my knees called to know what I was doing. I told him I was asking my God to send me some one to help me mend my barrow. The man then said, "Your God has certainly heard you this time for I'm a carpenter and I have my tools with me, so come along." He mended my barrow and helped me down the hill. *Now I do know God answers prayer.*"

Before the man was seated, young Mrs. Dwan had risen. Putting the little baby she had been holding in the arms of the woman next to her, she stood erect with quiet dignity and speaking in a low but clear voice that all could hear, she said:

"Pastor, I too wish to tell how I know God answers prayer. The first days of these meetings I received such a great blessing I longed to help some one else to know Christ, but I had so many duties with my little children and my home I could not go out, so I just kept praying as I went about my work, 'Lord, make the people go to the Church,' over and over again. Now, hasn't He heard my prayers?" And with a look of triumph she waved her hand first to the women's side and then to the men's, saying as she did so,—"Look there, and there!" The building was packed, aisles, window seats, even the windows were banked with faces, all listening quietly and attentively.

And now the closing scene. The day following the above-mentioned meetings, a number of Christians and a crowd of not unsympathetic villagers, gathered about Dr. Dwan's grave and erected to his memory a stone slab. Well might it have recorded on it that his path had been "by way of the Cross," from his first Gleam of the true Light to his entrance into the Glory beyond.

SKETCH II

Characters From One Village

Part 1—WANG-EE.
Part 2—WANG-EE'S NEIGHBORS.

Characters From One Village

Part I. WANG-EE.

The large and prosperous village of Ta-kwan-chwang is situated twelve miles southeast of Changte. As in most villages in China it had its best, or head-man, and its worst character—the leader of the worst element. In this case the former was Wang-ee; the latter a man named Liang.

In December of —, a Men's Bible Class was being conducted at the main station by Mr. M—— when to the surprise of all, this notoriously bad Liang was led in by one of the Christians who begged that he might be permitted to join the class as he was breaking off opium and wanted to be a good man. As the days passed poor Liang seemed incapable of taking in anything. He slept most of the time, would fall asleep the moment Mr. M—— began speaking, and his snores, to say the least, were most disturbing.

At last the missionary's patience became exhausted when an unusually loud snore reached his ears. Liang was told he had better leave as his presence was "useless to himself and disturbing to others." The man returned home apparently much crestfallen, and all thought he would never return; but a deeper work than others knew of had begun in him. On his return home his changed life became the talk of the village. Wang-ee, the headman, who was probably the wealthiest farmer in the region, heard of Liang's becoming a Christian, and of his wonderfully changed life. He talked with Liang and soon became interested. The Missionary, Mr. G——, hearing of the movement in this village, was preparing to pay them a visit when he received the following letter from Wang-ee.

"Honorable teacher Keo,—I hear you are planning to visit me,—do not come! When I get one hundred others to believe as I do I will come to you

—not before."

This message awakened much interest in the man, and day by day he was remembered in prayer. Several weeks passed when one day Wang-ee appeared at the missionary's door,—a typical, burly, well-to-do farmer. He lost no time in coming to his point. The first greetings over, he said, "I want to see through your home. May I?" The missionary led him through each room. The sewing machine puzzled him—not till it had been opened and examined inside would he believe but that a witch had made such stitches. When at last the kitchen was reached Wang-ee turned and said abruptly, "but is there nothing more?"

"No," replied Mr. G———, "nothing except the cellar."

"The cellar!" Wang-ee exclaimed, "why that is what I wanted to see most of all." Down they went. Then he began a vigorous search, the book boxes, then the coal and inside of the furnace was examined, then, when apparently satisfied, he faced the missionary, saying:

"Well, we Chinese are liars. A neighbor of mine told me he had seen in your cellar great crocks filled with children's flesh salted down."

The two returned to the study, when a long and earnest talk followed, at the close of which Wang-ee asked to have his name recorded as a probationer.

Some days later Wang-ee reappeared leading a large band of the chief men of his village. These he insisted on personally conducting through the house. On reaching the cellar Wang-ee became much excited. "Now look everywhere," he urged, "look now, see if there are any of those dead children you told me of. Will you ever lie to me about these missionaries again?" The men seemed very humble and not at all resentful. Later Wang-ee took them all into the city and treated them to a good dinner before returning home.

Nor was this all. A few days passed when again Wang-ee appeared—this time with a large wheeled cart drawn by six mules, and loaded down with women, all the women he could coax to come. These he led through the same process of enlightenment as the men. This time Wang-ee's face was a study, beaming as it was with delight as he saw the women's fears giving way to astonishment and delight at what they saw. With one or two exceptions all of these women became Christians. Within a very short time a flourishing little church existed in Wang-ee's village. Year by year the church grew till the cloudburst of 1900. Most, if not all the Christians

13

suffered in that terrible time of persecution,—Wang-ee lost heavily,—animals and grain were stolen, his life threatened, but he remained faithful.

* * *

The storm passed. The missionaries returned, work was reorganized. The Chinese Government ordered indemnity to be given to the Christians for their losses. Then, like many others, Wang-ee, though brave and faithful in peril and persecution, *fell* under prosperity. He gave in false estimates of his losses and received in proportion. God knew, though the missionaries did not. Year by year the church at Ta-kwau-chwang declined.

Then came a time of wonderful revival at Changte. Wang-ee sent his son to the meetings. The missionary missed his old friend and sent the son home to bring his father. When Wang-ee arrived he met Mr. G—— with, "Why did you send for me? I am too old and, anyway, I've no sins to confess."

That night poor Wang-ee seemed shaken as by a tempest. Hour after hour he wept. Those in the same room with him knew not what to do—for Wang-ee would say nothing. When morning came Wang-ee sent a message to Mr. G——, saying, "Oh, Pastor, give me a chance to confess before the meeting, I can't bear this, I will burst." The missionary met Wang-ee a little later near the church door. With their arms around each other, and tears flowing freely they entered the building. Reaching the platform Wang-ee cast himself down on his knees weeping bitterly. For several moments nothing could be heard but the man's sobs and sympathetic weeping throughout the audience. At last he made a full confession. He told how the church had gone down, down, and how when the missionary would question him as to the cause he would reply, "The time for blessing has not come."

He took the whole blame upon himself. He said it was not until he had come to the meetings that his eyes had been opened to the fact that he had been deceiving himself and trying to deceive God and man. He promised full restitution and kept his promise.

From that time Wang-ee's Christian character grew more and more in the likeness of his Master. He is now an old man of well-nigh eighty, ready for the call—beloved and honored by his fellow-Christians and surrounded by his family to the fourth generation.

Part II. WANG-EE's NEIGHBORS.

14

The great plain of North-Central China stretches for six hundred miles North and South. The villages are for the most part as thick as the homesteads in the more thickly populated districts of Western Ontario.

It was while visiting in one of these villages, Ta-kwan-chwang, that the writer came to know and love the characters sketched here.

First there comes to mind Wang-ee's aunt, the leading woman of her class, the one who chaperoned the women's party on their first visit to the missionary's home. She was the first woman to be baptized and was always for years, till "called Home," the one who most delighted in extending to us the hospitality of her home.

Then there was Wang-ee's gentle frail little wife, a striking contrast to the strong-minded, masterful personality of the aunt. This little woman seemed to spend her time sitting on a low stool in front of the great family caldron or pot in which the food was cooked. As she fed the fire with long, dried corn-stalks she directed her household, her sons and daughters-in-law, her grand-children, and later even great grand-children, not in the loud and stormy tones usually heard in heathen homes, but with a quiet dignity and self-command which often astonished the writer. What a monotonous life hers was! Day after day, year after year the same! No summer holidays for her! Was it much wonder she appeared always like a worn-out, tired-out human machine? Her faith was the faith of a little child, but she seemed incapable of fixing her mind on *herself*, so long and systematically had she thought of others. She, too, has passed on.

Then there comes Mrs. Lee—one of the first to accept Christ. Long standing eye trouble was fast destroying her eyesight, to save which she came to the women's hospital at Changte. Her one earnest request was that she might be permitted to hold the writer's hand during the operation, which was performed without chloroform. When all was over, she rose and said, "Oh, Jesus was beside me through it all."

Among the first converts in this village were two women, widows of two brothers. For years these women had never allowed the burning incense to become extinguished before the family tablets. They were both earnest devotees of a heathen religious sect. These women accepted Christ as their Saviour at the same time.

The elder whom we called Sung-ta-sao had a wonderful answer to prayer early in her Christian life. A young nephew whom she was bringing up as her own (she was childless) became critically ill with enlarged spleen, a

15

terribly fatal disease. Hearing of another Christian having had her child restored to health in answer to prayer when the doctor had pronounced him past hope, she gave herself to prayer for her nephew who was completely restored. This proof of the reality and power of God made a deep impression on the band of young Christians.

It was the second Mrs. Sung, however, who was next to Wang-ee himself, *the* character of the village. I shall not attempt to describe her appearance, especially as she looked when in winter garb, her clothes being quite as heavily wadded as a bed quilt, but undoubtedly she could truthfully say as another old lady said when seeing her photo for the first time, "I'm certainly the most unbeautifulest woman under heaven."

From the time of her conversion she was eager to preach the Gospel, but her *appearance* was against her. Miss M—— tried again and again to use her as a Bible woman. Then I tried her, but in vain. She could not hold an audience for five minutes. And yet of all our Christian women she was the most earnest. She could support herself and was entirely free, being motherless, so she had to return home, and for years did what she could in her own region. Then one day she came to our lady doctor and begged that she might have a place to spread her bed so that she might work among the women patients and try to lead them to Jesus.

The doctor hesitated, knowing the merriment her appearance caused, but decided to try her. That was more than three years ago, and Mrs. Sung is still working faithfully among the patients. She found her "nook." She keeps herself, and is as happy as the day is long in teaching the women to pray and learn the simple Gospel leaflets. Her face so shines with joy and contentment as to appear almost lovely to those who know her.

There are others worthy of being introduced to you, my reader, but there is room for only one more.

Mr. and Mrs. Wang-chang-ling were among the earliest believers. Mrs. Wang was slow to learn. How could she be otherwise, never having read a word in her life, accustomed to the hardest toil in the fields and in the home, her face and hands showing only too plainly what privation and hardship she had come through, and then at fifty years of age trying to master the Christian Catechism. It is no wonder she would sigh and say, "I shall *never* learn to read," and then in her characteristic way look up and say, "But never mind, I can *pray* anyway!" She always had a bright smile of welcome, and would take one's hand and thank us again and again for coming.

Then the Boxer uprising came. Both Mr. and Mrs. Wang-Chang-ling suffered greatly. The Boxers came to their home, bound and carried off the husband. For days the wife knew not what had become of him. He suffered much at the hands of his captors, but finally made his escape. For three months he was driven from place to place, until nigh unto death, but as he testified God never left him, and always provided a way of escape and raised up friends when most needed and least expected.

While he was fleeing for his life his wife suffered too. The soldiers came, bound her, and carried her off to the Changte official. She afterwards testified that when being taken away thus, not knowing but that even death awaited her, she felt so happy she could not keep from singing. She was beaten two hundred blows to make her tell where her husband was. Then her finger was twisted, but she remained firm and true through it all. On our return in 19— the writer cannot forget, though many years have since passed, the joy of meeting these dear people, but it was but a short meeting. Both husband and wife died shortly after within a few days of each other, both witnessing triumphantly the hope of the Christians to the Life Everlasting.

"They shall hunger no more, neither thirst any more; neither shall the sun light on them nor any heat. For the Lamb which is in the midst of the throne shall feed them, and shall lead them into living fountains of waters: and God shall wipe away all tears from their eyes."

SKETCH III

The Man Who Proved God

"Him that honoreth Me I will honor."

The Man Who Proved God

"Him that honoreth Me I will honor."

The last of a long stream of patients had just gone. It was five o'clock and the tired doctor turned his face once more towards the rear of the Mission Compound, where lay his beloved garden, his one source of relaxation after a day spent in fighting disease and death.

To-day as he reached the inner gate, something, shall we not more truly say, *Someone*, seemed to make him turn about, and he retraced his steps, he knew not why; back past the dispensary door he went till he had reached the main gateway.

* * *

17

Two men carrying a stretcher upon which lay a sick man, came staggering along the road leading past the Mission premises. They were evidently not in the best of humor, for as they mopped their streaming brows, frequent oaths escaped them. Suddenly, as the Mission gate was reached, they dropped their burden with a cruel thud upon the ground, for both bearers had caught sight of the foreigner coming up to the gate. This was by far too interesting a sight to miss, so both men squatted down opposite the gate to rest while they watched with keenest interest this foreign man of whom they had heard many wonderful stories, but whom they had never seen.

The doctor, with true instinct, walked straight to the sick man and raised the cloth covering his face. Hardened as he was to all kinds of "cases," what he saw evidently shocked him, for he gave an exclamation of surprise.

"Where are you taking him?" he asked the bearers.

"Home," was the reply.

"But do you know he will certainly die?"

"That's certain," was the answer. "We were just considering as we came up whether we would not *just bury him as he is*, for neither of us cares to stand for forty *li* more (14 miles) what we have stood those last forty *li*."

The doctor knew well it meant for him many months of hard fighting with a most loathsome disease, with only a bare chance of success, yet in the spirit of his Master he did not hesitate but said, "Give him to me. If he can be saved, I'll save him. If he dies, he will have proper burial." After consulting together for a few moments the men turned to the doctor and said, "You can have him." So the man was carried into the hospital.

The following day, at the missionaries' noon prayer-meeting much interest was roused as the doctor told of his strange leading the day before and of the result. Earnest prayer rose for Lu Yung Kwan, the sick man, whose past history made his case seem the more hopeless. He had been a professional juggler (about as low in the scale as one could well get), and had lived a very depraved life.

The history of the year that followed could better be told by the doctor or his colleague who worked, rather fought for the man's salvation, both soul and body. But the day came when he went from the Mission Hospital healed in body and a professed follower of the Lord Jesus Christ.

18

Twice in the months that followed Lu Yung Kwan fell; the second time he went back to his old life so deep and so long his Mission friends almost despaired of him. But God had mercy on him, and he rose as the future proved, "*a new creation*" in Christ Jesus.

Barely has there been a more striking illustration of Paul's words, "Put off the old man with his deeds," than Lu Yung Kwan's after life. He opened a small bakery and food shop where many passed to and fro with their barrows of coal, the coal pits being in the region. He was the only Christian in the region. On his counter was always a place for Christian books and tracts; and he was ever on the alert to take advantage of the curiosity and interest these awakened, and to bear witness to what the Lord had done for him.

From the first opening of his business he determined to obey the injunction of Malachi 3:10,—"Bring ye the whole tithe ... and prove me now ... saith Jehovah of Hosts, if I will not open you the windows of heaven, and pour you out a blessing, that there shall not be room enough to receive it." He not only gave a tithe of all he made to the Lord, but put aside for Him one cash in every hundred, "Just to bless the rest."

He married a bright Christian girl, who proved herself a true helpmeet to him. Four children came to bless their home; one girl whom they named Glory, and three boys, Paul, Luke and Joseph.

One day when visiting near their home, the writer asked the second boy, whom she met on the street, his name. He answered, "My name is the Gospel according to Luke!"

It is not too much to say that the Lord prospered this man in all that he did. As an example of this:—One year almost famine conditions prevailed through Lu Yung Kwan's region, when the missionary paid a visit to the little band of Christians which had gathered around this faithful witnesser to the Truth.

One day Mr. Lu and the Missionary went for a walk. Noticing a fine field of wheat in striking contrast to the almost dead fields of grain surrounding it, the missionary asked to whom it belonged. Mr. Lu replied that it was his, and quietly remarked, "That is how the Lord blesses me."

Some time later when the writer was visiting near his home, Mr. Lu called upon her when he told her the story of his life. One thing he said was, "I know now why the Lord allowed me to fall twice. I was too self-confident. I had to learn that Christ must be all and I nothing."

19

Only a few months later the call came to meet his Master. He glorified the Lord in his death as in his life; he died in full assurance of Eternal Life. He left behind his widow and children comfortably provided for, and a band of Christians to testify to God's faithfulness in opening as He had promised "windows of blessing" for the man who dared to "prove" Him.

* * *

Before closing this sketch I would like to record an incident which occurred some years after her husband's death in which Mrs. Lu proved to be a veritable God-send to the writer. To be understood the story must be told somewhat in detail.

Returning to our station from an unusually strenuous autumn's touring, I planned as usual to give the month of December to the children's sewing, so as to leave January free for a Woman's Bible Training Class, but my health broke down and strive as I could scarcely any headway was made with thirty-five or forty garments which had to be made by the time the children returned to their school in Chefoo. By the 18th of December the January class had to be cancelled and word was sent to all the women who were to attend with one exception—Mrs. Lu, and she was *overlooked*!

As the days passed the burden of the almost untouched sewing became very great till I was forced to cry to the Lord for a way out of the difficulty. On December 28th, while leading the Chinese Woman's Prayer meeting, I noticed Mrs. Lu in the audience and at once knew she had come from her distant home over rough mountain roads with her little child for the class which was cancelled. Feeling very sorry for the thoughtlessness which had given her the needless trouble and expense I invited her to my home and gave her some money for a barrow to take herself and child home the following day. I then sat down to the sewing machine while Mrs. Lu stood beside and watched. In a few moments she said, "You look very tired. Let me run the machine for you." I looked at her in amazement, and said, "You run the machine? Why you don't know how."

"Yes I do," she replied. "I joined a band of women in our village and had a machine brought and we all learned to run it. Just try me."

As I gave her first easy and then more and more difficult things to do and saw how she did them perfectly, I felt awed at the plainness of God's leading, for there was only one other Chinese woman, as far as I knew, in our whole Changte field who could run the sewing machine. But again came a test of faith, for when I asked her to stay and help me with the sewing she replied that she must return home on the morrow. Puzzled and disappointed I could only again ask the Lord to undertake, and again I proved His faithfulness. That night a fierce storm, lasting several days, came on, making the roads quite impassable. Mrs. Lu, finding herself storm-tied, gladly gave all her time to me. The roads remained impassable for a whole month, during which time all the sewing was finished and I had not needed to sit down to the machine once!

"They shall abundantly utter the memory of Thy great Goodness."

SKETCH IV

Opening a New Station

Part 1—THE MISSIONARY'S HOME.
Part 2—AS RAIN FROM A CLEAR SKY.
Part 3—SOWING BEFORE THE STORM.

Opening a New Station

Part I. THE MISSIONARY'S HOME.

Wee Nell's eyes had closed at last, and the tired mother rising from the child's bedside crossed the cement floor to the adjoining room, where a boy of six was busily engaged drawing on a blackboard to the evident delight of his little sister.

"My boy," said his mother, "baby has just gone to sleep and must not be disturbed. These constant crowds of women keep her from proper rest, so run out with your little sister to the back compound and play."

As the children disappeared, the mother prepared to cut out some little garments, but scarcely had she taken scissors in hand when suddenly she laid them down again, and stood listening. In the distance could be heard the noisy shouts of a band of cotton gleaners. "Would they come in?" she asked herself. Then, as they could be heard sweeping through the front gateway, she pushed her work to one side exclaiming aloud, "Oh, dear, dear, how can I ever get the children's clothes made! If only a rainy day would come I might get something made."

"Patience, patience," her husband's voice came through the study door. "These crowds will not last indefinitely, so do your best to reach them while you may." Before he had finished speaking his wife's voice could be heard greeting the crowd in the courtyard.

21

"Please sit down here in the shade and rest, do sit down, see, here are benches and mats," she urged as they crowded about her, a wild unruly mob.

"We have come to see," cried a dozen voices at once.

"I know you have," she replied, trying to speak so as not to waken the baby and yet be heard above the din of voices. "I really cannot let you inside unless you first sit down and listen to what I have to say." Then as they still hesitated she continued, "If you will sit down and listen, I will promise to let you inside and show you everything." This promise had the desired effect—down they sat on mats, some on benches,—a few timid ones kept close to the gate so as to be ready to flee at the first approach of danger! As the mother tried to tell them why she had come—of a Saviour from sin—of a hope after death, some listened intently and seemed to get a gleam of light, but for the most part the crowd was restless and keen only to get inside the house about which they had heard so many strange stories. At last baby Nell wakened, and making the fact known by lusty cries, gave the women the opportunity they desired.

As the mother ran to her little one the crowd of forty or fifty women and children pressed in after her. With the baby in her arms the mother faithfully kept her promise. Nothing escaped their curious eyes—beds were turned back, drawers opened, sewing machine examined, and organ played before they appeared satisfied. Whereupon they rushed off as quickly as they had come, saying to one another, "The foreign devil woman does not seem as bad as people say she is." Others said, "But who knows, you can never judge by appearances!" Half an hour later the husband returned from the man's preaching to find his wife in tears.

"Why, what's wrong?" he asked.

"Oh, everything," his wife replied between her sobs. "I just can't bear it. You don't know how they despise me and what terrible things they are saying. Besides when I came back to my work I found they had carried off my last pair of scissors and part of the material I was making a dress of. That is not all. The cook has just been in to say that several teaspoons are missing."

"Tut, tut," replied her husband, man-like. "That's nothing. Why they are only *things* anyway!"

A few days later came the missionary's turn to need sympathy. He came in from the front looking pale and apparently quite worn out.

"I tell you what, wife," he said, "I cannot stand this strain much longer without help! If I only had a good preacher to put in charge of the preaching hall, I could get along; but with lime to weigh, bricks to count, wood and timber to measure, and all the Mission accounts to keep, besides the oversight of all these workmen, and the preaching to these crowds of men that are coming daily, well—I just must get help."

He went into his study, but returned a moment later with an open Bible in his hand. Pointing to these words, "My God shall supply all your need," he said, "Wife, do we really believe this? If we do, then let us join in asking God to meet this pressing need of ours for an evangelist."

"But how is it possible," returned his wife. "We have not got even one convert yet, and have promised the other stations not to ask help of them as they are undermanned?"

"True, but God is able to fulfil His own promises."

As the husband prayed, the wife thought, "but, oh, how can help come. *It is as if we were praying for rain from a clear sky.*"

Two days later the answer did come,—not, indeed, as they expected, but above all they could have thought. The story of this must be left for our next sketch.

Part II. AS RAIN FROM A CLEAR SKY.

"Call upon me in the day of trouble and I will deliver thee, and thou shalt glorify me."

A poor broken opium slave lay on a kang or brick bed with only a thin straw mat between his emaciated form and the cold bricks. His livid color, with the peculiar dark shade of the moderate opium user, his sunken cheeks and labored breathing, all betokened the man had reached the stage when only a miracle could save him. Beside him stood a missionary, who was saying earnestly as he laid his hand kindly on the man's shoulder:

"Wang Pu Lin, I tell you God *can* save you."

"No, no, Pastor," the man replied sadly, "It's no use. I've tried and failed too often. I believe all you preach, but what is the use of believing when this opium binds me as with iron chains? Even Pastor Hsi's Refuge failed to cure me. No no, don't waste your time on me. I'm beyond hope." And the man turned again to his opium.

But the missionary was not the kind to be so easily rebuffed. The next day

23

found Wang Pu Lin and the missionary on the Mission court en route for the station of Chu Wang.

For ten awful days Wang Pu Lin's body, mind and soul hung in the balance. The missionaries united in doing all that was possible to relieve the man's agonies. It was on the tenth night the crisis came. Many times later Wang Pu Lin told how that night he went out when in bitter agony into the darkness. To his distorted brain there appeared to him a horrible being urging him to jump the wall and get relief once more in opium. As he stood wavering a voice seemed to call to him, "Wang Fu Lin, Wang Fu Lin, beware! Yield now and you are lost." As he heard this voice he made one desperate effort, crying aloud, "Oh, God, help me. I will die rather than yield." Staggering back to his brick bed he threw himself upon it and slept till morning. He wakened, as the future proved, a new and victorious man.

* * *

Three years passed. The missionary at the new station is facing the crisis described in our last sketch. Help must come in the shape of an evangelist, or he would break down. The spiritual wireless is set in motion. The cry for aid is heard. And help is sent truly *as rain from a clear sky.*

During the three years since his deliverance from the opium, Wang Fu Lin and his family had had a bitter struggle for existence. As a Christian he could no longer make a living by street story telling and the keeping of low opium dives, and every effort to get honest employment had failed. At last he determined to seek a position in the city of Changte, to reach which he must needs pass by the Mission where the missionary was then facing his crisis.

Wang Fu Lin called on the missionary as he was passing. But no one could have looked less like an answer to their prayers. Still fearfully emaciated, racked with a cough which ere long would end his life, dressed in almost beggar rags, the poor fellow presented a pitiable spectacle. But "the Lord seeth not as man seeth."

After consulting together the missionary and his wife determined to try him for a few days—for he could at least testify to the power of God to change and keep the lowest opium slave. Within an hour or two of his entering the Mission gate, apparently a beggar, Wang Fu Lin was cleansed and clothed in a Chinese outfit of the missionary's, and was seated in the men's chapel preaching to a crowded audience.

From that very first day of his ministry, there was no doubt of his being a messenger sent by God. He had in a wonderful degree the power and unction of the Holy Spirit. He had natural gifts as a speaker, and these had been developed during the many years of street story telling. Now all was consecrated to the one object—the winning of souls to Christ. He seemed to be conscious that his time was short, and always spoke as "a dying man to dying men." From the very first men were won to Christ; the first being a native doctor of some note, the second a wealthy land owner.

For three years during those early days of stress and strain, he was spared to help in laying the foundations of the Changte Church. Then God took him. Though more than twenty years have passed since his death, he is still remembered and spoken of as the Spirit-filled preacher.

Part III. SOWING BEFORE THE STORM.

The five years between 1895 and 1900 were years fraught with much danger and many difficulties to the missionaries at the new station at Changte. The anti-foreign, anti-missionary attitude of the people was hard to live down. It became quite a common thing for the missionary to be called hastily to the front to quiet a threatening crowd.

On one occasion the Mission premises were practically surrounded by an unruly mob and for many hours the missionaries were in imminent peril. One thing helped greatly in living this danger period down safely. The missionaries of whom I have already written had moved from the poor, unhealthy Chinese house with the cement floor into a semi-foreign house, the first of the kind to be built in that region. As this house was being built they feared it might prove a barrier between themselves and the Chinese, and perhaps hinder the progress of the work which had begun to be very encouraging, so they prayed that God would make their new home a blessing and a means of reaching the people still more, and like so many of our prayers they came to see the answer lay largely with themselves—so they determined to allow all who wished, to see through their home. Many thousands took advantage of this permission. The high water mark in numbers was reached when eighteen hundred and thirty-five *men* passed through the missionary's home in one day. Many hundreds of women were received that same day by the wife and her colleague in the work. On ordinary occasions the missionary had his wife play the organ for the bands of men he led through, but on this particular occasion she was too much engaged with the women to do so. The missionary therefore was forced to be his own organist. Though he did not know one note from

25

another, he could at least pull out all the stops, lay his hands on as many notes as possible, and pump the bellows vigorously. The result called forth from admiring crowds the gratifying remark, "Why he plays better than his wife!" The Gospel was faithfully proclaimed to all who came. The missionaries soon began to see good fruit from this plan of reaching the people.

During the second year at Changte hundreds of students had come to the city for the tri-annual government examinations. Many of these visited and showed plainly their anti-foreign attitude—sometimes causing quite serious trouble.

Before the next examinations came round, three years later, the missionary was well prepared for them. At first they came as before full of self-satisfied convictions that they were quite superior representatives of the most superior race. Curiosity alone led them to the foreigner's home. But no sooner would they catch sight of the large astronomical charts on the missionary's study wall than their attitude invariably changed. The missionary knew well the importance of reserving his ammunition till the right moment! The proudest of those scholars in face of those charts became like children.

As the man of God led them (at their own request) step by step on into the wonders of creation of which they knew nothing—often would come the cry, "Teacher stop, have pity on us—you make us feel like the man in the well who thought he saw the whole heavens!"

The change that came over hundreds of these students was truly remarkable. Just one instance of the fruit of this work. The missionary was touring far west of Changte and stayed with his party at a certain inn. The inn-keeper when asked for his bill as the party was leaving replied —"Honorable teacher, I could not accept anything from you. My son was at the recent examinations at Changte and has told me of his visit to your home and what you are doing for our people!"

One day early in 19— three of the missionary's children were gathered in front of a curious looking chart tacked on the wall of the study. It was a rough map of the Changte field, and over parts of the chart were red dots. The eldest child was counting those red spots and had reached to forty-nine when his father entered.

"Oh, father," cried the boy, "just look, there are almost fifty red places."

"Yes," said his father, "And do you know dear children that every red mark means a place where one or more Christians are, and where the light of the Gospel that can save men has entered?"

"Oh, won't it be lovely, father, when the whole map is red?" said a sweet fair-haired little girl as she threw her arms about her father's neck.

Oh kind Heavenly Father, who withheld from Thy children's human sight what Thou knewest was so soon to come upon them!

A few short weeks after the above scene the spirit of the little fair-haired child had returned to the God who gave it, the missionaries even fleeing before their would-be murderers—the Chinese Christians scattered. Many throughout China, both missionaries and Chinese Christians were witnessing a good confession even to cruel death for Christ's sake.

So the blood of the martyrs became in China, as in the early times, the seed of the Christian Church in China.

SKETCH V

Testing God

A True Incident.

Testing God

A TRUE INCIDENT.

"*Faith steps out on the seeming void and finds the Rock beneath.*"

Few in the home-land have any just conception of what it means for a missionary's wife with little children to engage in aggressive evangelistic effort for the reaching of her heathen sisters. The following sketch which is true in every detail may serve to illustrate what a missionary mother must face when engaging in such work.

* * *

"I simply cannot, dare not, go," the wife was saying as her husband stood before her with a Chinese letter in his hand. "The letter states plainly that an epidemic of smallpox has broken out in the very place we planned to go to. If it were not for baby I would gladly go; but supposing he should later take the smallpox and die?" and her voice ended with a sudden break. "But," replied her husband, "I am perfectly sure that if we definitely trust Him for the child God will not let him come to harm. The Christians are all expecting us, and would it be right to show the white feather at the first appearance of danger? How can we tell the Chinese to trust God if we do

27

not?"

For an hour or more the mother went through a bitter struggle between her fears for her child and an impelling sense of duty towards her heathen sisters. At last she determined to go, but with fear and trembling lest the child should get the smallpox.

The following evening after bumping (the only word to express the movement) for eight hours in a springless cart over hills and stony roads, the missionaries reached the village of Hopei. Some distance outside the village a few Christians were awaiting their arrival and escorted them through the darkness to the Inn—each one anxious to help in getting their guests settled. One carried the roll of bedding—two others the food box, still another sought to get possession of the baby, but the mother feared to part with him. Everything was piled in a promiscuous heap on the large brick platform which took up about half of the room which they were told was to be their living-room and women's preaching place as well. The room was certainly not inviting; the roof was broken in (ceiling there was none), the walls were black with the soot and dirt of generations, and hard uneven lumpy earth did for floors. Furniture, there was none—not even a table or chair.

The mother's first question was "where can I keep the baby?" For answer she was led to an opening in the wall beyond which was a mud hole just large enough to spread their bedding, but at the further end were several great rat holes! A sudden desperate fear for her child took possession of the mother, but pride kept her from letting her husband know her fears.

Early the following morning the women and children from the surrounding country began crowding in. By nine o'clock the room was packed to suffocation with a great crowd outside trying to get in. All were clamoring to see and feel the foreign woman and her child. These women knew absolutely nothing of the Gospel, and as the missionary mother looked into their rough, ignorant, sensual faces and thought how she had even risked the life of her precious child to come to them, a great yearning came into her heart to be used of God to bring light to their dark minds. For many hours a day she and her faithful Bible woman preached to the ever changing crowd. Sometimes they were both in despair at the crush and confusion. Constantly could be seen children marked with smallpox carried in their mother's arms. At times the atmosphere was so over-powering the mother could only cry to God to keep her from fainting.

Though early in May the weather was very warm, and the husband

28

continually had the easier time for he had both light and air preaching as he did in the open court.

All through the week the baby had stood the confinement and conditions wonderfully. When not asleep he would delight and win the women by his happy ways. But Saturday morning found him ill and feverish, lying listless in his mother's arms. The mother was for at once rushing home with him, but her husband gently rebuked her lack of faith, and reminded her of their promise to hold a communion service at a distant village on the morrow.

Before day-break the next morning, Sunday, all the missionary's party was astir, and as the dawn was breaking they filed out of the yard through the quiet deserted streets into the country, following a winding mountain path. When at last the summit of quite a high hill was reached, the missionary sent the rest of the party on ahead, while he and his wife sat down with their sleeping child. For a long time neither could break the silence, their hearts were too full. Never will either forget the peace and beauty of that hour. It was all intensified by the contrast with what they had left behind. The mother could only think with horror of the darkness and dirt, sin and suffering, turmoil and unspeakable degradation in which they had lived for those six days. But now it seemed as if they were in heaven itself. Oh, the beauty of that scene! To the east the sun was just appearing in all its height of glory. To the north, south, and west, rose mountains and hills still in shadow, except for the tipping of the coming sun whose herald of glory lit up the eastern sky and plain which stretched out before them as far as the eye could reach.

It seemed there on that hill-top alone with God so easy to trust for the little one who was still feverish and ill. But all too soon, as it seemed, they had to leave that quiet spot and go down into the valley—to the noise and confusion of the village where their Sabbath ministry lay. The following morning early they once more turned their faces homeward, and as the mother saw the bright, happy smile on her child's face, the fever gone, she pressed him to her with joy and thankfulness, and there arose in her heart a cry for forgiveness that she had been so faithless and unbelieving.

> This cruel self, oh how it strives
> And works within my breast,
> How many subtle forms it takes
> * * * *
> As if it were not *safe* to rest

29

And venture *all* on Thee."

As years passed the mother's faith did grow, but it was on *God's faithfulness* until she learnt it *was safe* to venture *all* on Him.

Dear fellow-mother in the homeland, as you realize from these lines something of what it costs a mother in China to step out from her home to save her Chinese sisters, ask yourself "Could *I* do it?" Oh, my sisters, criticize less and pray more for the missionary mothers of China.

SKETCH VI

A Christian General

Hope for China's Soldiers.

A Christian General

HOPE FOR CHINA'S SOLDIERS.

(The following letter was written on board river steamer immediately at the close of the visit to General Feng's camp.)

On Board Yangtze Steamer,

September 2, 1919.

Dear Home Friends:

About the beginning of July, a very urgent message reached Doctor Goforth from General Feng of Chang-teh, Hunan, asking for a "mission" among his troops. The only possible time he had to give was the last week of August, and the meetings were arranged for this time. Later the General telegraphed for me to come for meetings among the 70 or 80 officers' wives.

When the time drew near that we should have to leave Chi Kung Shan for Chang-teh, word came that cholera was raging at places along the railway. Then the heat became so intense I was tempted to listen to some who urged me not to go. But as I hesitated, I was led to Ecclesiastes 11:4—"He that observeth the wind shall not sow, and he that regardeth the clouds shall not reap." How could I refuse to go, in face of such a text? If I had not gone, what I would have missed!

The journey of one day by train and three by steamer was extremely hot. It was as if we were in a Turkish bath day and night. We slept at night on the deck of the steamer. On Sunday afternoon, Aug. 24th, we reached the house of Mr. Caswell of the Holiness Mission. It was amusing to read the General's letter written in English by his Chinese English Teacher, in which he said to Mr. Caswell, "I beg you to prepare the treatment for their coming."

General Feng called within an hour of our arrival. He is over six feet tall, and every inch a General, yet without a trace of the bombast so often seen in the higher-class Chinese. His manner is a curious and striking mixture of humility, dignity, and quiet power; he has a handsome, good face. He at once impresses one as true and sincere, a man to be trusted. He has been a Christian for six years.

THE STORY OF HIS CONVERSION.

The story of his conversion is most interesting, but it is too long to give in detail. In brief, it is as follows:—When a young fellow of sixteen, he joined the army. Shortly after, the Boxer Uprising broke out. He was among those sent to put down the Boxers at Pao-ting-fu, but his commanding officer was really in league with them. One day he stood in a mission courtyard when the Boxers came in. A single lady missionary came out to meet them, and pleaded for her own life and the lives of the others with her, and with great power recounted what she and others had been doing for their people. What she said touched the young soldier. She and the others were spared then, but he heard that they were all beheaded later.

Soon after, he was taken ill and treated at the mission hospital in Peking. On leaving, he wanted to give money; but the doctor said. "If you are truly grateful for what we have done for you, then all I ask of you is to remember that there is our God in heaven Who loves you." Later, he was again obliged to go to hospital for treatment at a place far distant from the first one. Here the doctor, on his leaving, said almost exactly the same words—"Remember there is a God in heaven Who loves you."

Some time after this, the future General was in Peking when Dr. Mott was holding meetings. He heard Dr. Mott, was much impressed, signed one of the cards, and joined a Bible Study Class. He was thus definitely started on the right road; and, though other circumstances combined to lead him to take an out-and-out stand, he dated the beginning of his Christian life from Dr. Mott's visit.

THE GENERAL'S WORK.

Before coming here to Chang-teh, we had heard a great deal of what marvels the General had accomplished in the year he has been here; but what we have seen surpasses what we heard. General Feng has the welfare of his soldiers, both body and soul, at heart. This is seen by the fact that he has put down vice of all kinds. All bad resorts and their inmates are removed far from the camp. No smoking, drinking, gambling, or opium is allowed. The officers, including himself, dress in the plainest gray cotton. Even the officers' wives are not allowed to wear silks, but just plain cotton. No foot-binding is allowed.

The General has arranged all sorts of athletic sports for officers and men. There is a fine reading room; the illiterate are taught to read. There is a school for officers' wives taught by a Christian lady, the wife of one of the officers and a graduate of the Peking Girls' School. There is an industrial school for women; also an industrial school for men who are nearing the age limit of the army, to teach them ways of earning a livelihood.

Christian worship is taught and encouraged in every way. One morning Dr. Goforth and I had occasion to pass through several courtyards of the men's quarters just at breakfast time. As we passed along, we saw the men in groups standing before the food singing their morning hymn of thanksgiving. And we were told by the missionaries living near the camp that every evening they can hear the soldiers singing their evening hymn. Sometimes it is, "Oh, come to my heart Lord Jesus; there is room in my heart for Thee"—or "Pass me not, O gentle Saviour." As the soldiers march along the street, they sing Christian hymns, one of the favorites for marching being "Onward, Christian Soldiers."

The General has a band, and also a choir; but I hardly know what to say about the quality of the singing and music generally. I can only give my impression of it as I heard them in the Assembly Hall at one of the meetings. The band, organ and men all start at once on the third stroke of the baton, no leading note being given. Every instrument in the band seemed to my ears to be tuned to a different key, and every man seemed to sing without the least regard for the key of his neighbor. All kept the tune, as far as I could hear, and all played or sang as loudly as they could bang, toot, or shout. The general effect was deafening, and to me almost appalling, for there were about 1,000 men and some twenty instruments engaged. When the General later called upon the choir of twenty men to sing by themselves with just the baby organ accompaniment, it was really delightful to listen to them. They sang very well indeed.

THE MISSION AND ITS RESULT.

And now as to the "Mission" we have just held. From the first, God has been very manifestly working. Twice every day Dr. Goforth has had an attentive and keenly interested audience of about 1,000 men, chiefly officers. At three of these meetings the wives were permitted to be present; but all the rest of the women's meetings were separate, when God gave me much help in speaking to them. At our last meeting, practically all the officers' wives present said they wished to follow the Lord Jesus.

At one of the last meetings for the men, General Feng broke down as he tried to pray. What seemed to affect him was the thought of his country. As soon as he could recover from his sobs, he stood up and, facing his officers, pleaded for his country—pleaded with them to join him in putting aside all mean motives, and think and work and pray for their country. One of his staff officers followed, praying earnestly, then one after the other of the officers, with sobs and tears cried to God on behalf of themselves and their country.

An old missionary who was present, and who described the scene to me, said he did not think there had ever been such a scene before when a general wept before his own officers, with all that followed. But the discipline was not broken by it; for when the General rose to leave, the audience rose as one man.

Dr. Goforth and General Feng went yesterday to a camp 23 miles away, where there are about 4,000 troops. Five hundred of these have already been baptized, and hundreds more are enquiring. A Christian Chinese gentleman, who has won a fine name, is to come to act as the General's chaplain and organize the work among the troops.

THE COMING MAN OF CHINA.

Many feel that General Feng is the coming man of China. His troops belong rightly to the north, but were sent down here to fight the Southern Army. General Feng, however, has made it clear to the Peking Government that he is willing and eager to fight the enemies of his country; but, unless forced to do so, he will not fight his own countrymen of the south. When the war was on, he telegraphed more than once to be sent to France; and when the situation looked very serious in Shantung a few months ago, General Feng was spoken of as the man to cope with the Japanese.

33

Surely it is a cause for most earnest praise to God that such a man is being raised up. The very fact that such wonderful possibilities lie before him, and that after all he is but human, should call forth definite prayer for him. China needs—oh, so terribly!—just such men. May God grant that General Feng be kept and used to save his country at this time of crisis.

July 24th, 1919.—Almost a year has passed since the above letter was written. Several thousands of General Feng's soldiers are now baptized and the splendid work continues. But as I write, civil war, which has been simmering for years, has now broken out in dead earnest, General Feng and his men are in the midst of the conflict and all are looking to him and his friend Wu-pei-fu to save the situation in this crisis.

SKETCH VII

A Chinese Nobleman

A Chinese Nobleman

As I review the life of the man of whom I am to write, two incidents of over thirty years ago come to mind. On our way to China one of our fellow-passengers was a man who had been in business twenty odd years in China. He declared there were no real Christians in China, that they were all "rice" Christians—followers of the foreigner for what they could get and so on. Practically all the passengers, except the missionaries heartily agreed with these statements. Later we heard the same thing repeated on the coast steamer. Shortly after reaching our destination a well-known resident of China, who had occupied for twenty-five years a responsible position in the "Customs" made such positive statements along the same line that the writer began to wonder if these things could be true. Six weeks later this accuser, and as I know now to be, cruel slanderer of the Christians had gone to meet his Judge—dying suddenly in his chair as the result of a vicious debauch!

It is now the writer's privilege to give testimonies after thirty years standing, to the genuineness of the Chinese Christian—here is one of them.

Twenty miles northeast of the Mission Station of Changteho lived a well-to-do banker and landowner named Chen-Lao-Jung. He was a man of most masterful personality. His old mother, to whom he was greatly devoted, had long been afflicted by attacks of what the Chinese called demon possession—which from all accounts exactly resembled those recorded in the Bible. Every heathen means had been used for her relief.

34

Witch doctors, necromancers, Buddhist priests, and others had used their arts upon her (some of these being very cruel), but the poor woman was "nothing better, but rather grew worse."

One day a Christian called when the woman was in a serious and violent condition. Mr. Chen asked Mr. Hsu, the Christian, to pray to his God for his mother, but the Christian replied, "I would gladly do so, but it is useless for me to pray to my God, who is the only true God, when you recognize so many other gods that are false. These household gods must first be destroyed: then I can pray." (Oh, that our home Christians would realize this too, *then* would *they* know the power of prayer).

After some demur Mr. Chen decided that he had tried these gods and they had failed him, now he would burn them rather than lose this opportunity of having his mother healed by the Christian God!

In face of the bitterest opposition from his family and neighbors he publicly burnt all the household gods. Then he and Mr. Hsu followed by all the family and a crowd of curious neighbors went into the mother's room where she lay foaming on the bed. Mr. Hsu first sang the hymn "Jesus loves me"—then prayed, then sang again.

Gradually the woman quieted down and before long was completely restored. Thus the Lord as of old answered prayer and delivered the woman from the terrible power which had had such a hold upon her. Her deliverance was so wonderful that all the family and some neighbors immediately accepted the Gospel.

Mr. Chen left his home and business for several weeks and came to the out-station where the writer and her husband were. Here he took the place of a little child. His humility, earnestness, and sincerity impressed us all. When he felt he had grasped the main truths of the Gospel he returned home realizing as few Christians seem to do, that he had been saved to save others. He at once started family worship, and prepared a building as a chapel and preaching hall—here he gathered and taught all who wished to learn. His whole family became out and out for Christ and soon neighbors were won. The first of these was a notable opium slave. The story in detail of the growth of Christianity in Mr. Chen's region would fill a volume, but space permits only the brief record of open outstanding facts.

About two years after Mr. Chen became a Christian the locusts came over the country in great numbers, eating all before them. Mr. Chen told his family that since they would all be busy fighting the locusts, family worship would for the time be given up. A few days later a fine boy in the family, about seven years of age, became paralyzed in one side and was unable to get off the kang (or brick bed). The following is Mr. Chen's own account of what followed.

"One day I was out in the fields fighting the locusts when I suddenly seemed to waken out of sleep. "Hsing Wu kuo lai" I cried aloud—'Why! *the connection is cut! The connection is cut!*' I hastened home and called all the family together. I told them to get down on their knees and confess with me our sin of *putting God aside*, that by doing so we had cut the connection with God, for God had said, 'Your iniquities have separated between you and your God and your sins have hid His face from you. Oh, Lord now that the connection is mended, won't you heal the little boy?' And as we prayed we heard the child get off the kang, and before we rose from our knees he was running around quite well."

Mr. Chen became a tower of strength to the missionary, who when obliged to be absent sometimes from that part of his field would commit the affairs of the Church into his hands. Did he get money for this, you ask. No—all his service was for love of his Lord.

Not many months ago this man stood bravely, grandly, one of the severest tests any Christian could be put to.

He had a very dear little daughter, a pretty, gentle, timid child of about nine years of age. This child was away from home when she was attacked by a young woman of violent temper, the daughter of another Christian. The child was struck several times with a heavy stick, and as she fled terrified was followed and struck again, it is believed, on the head, a few days later the child returned home, but could say little else than, "I'm afraid" over and over again. She sank rapidly and died; but before her death she told her father of the attack upon her. A few days later the writer received a most touching letter from Mr. Chen in which he reviewed the past—what he had been saved from—what Christ had been to him— then wrote as follows—

"Shepherd Mother—My heart is crushed, my little daughter is dead. I do not want the one who killed her to be punished. I only ask that you warn her so that other children shall not suffer as mine has done."

Those of us who know how exceedingly *revengeful* the Chinese are by nature will agree that one could scarcely find a more beautiful example of

36

the power and fruit of the Gospel of Jesus Christ than this.

SKETCH VIII

Mr. Doong

Mr. Doong

My husband and I with our children had settled down for a few weeks' stay at one of our out stations, when I noticed one morning at breakfast a strange man sweeping the yard. He looked such a queer bundle of incongruous clothes I could not make out if he were a teacher, a poor farmer, or a coolie. The man's face was so wrinkled and his shoulders so stooped he looked a much older man than his years, which could not have been more than fifty.

"Who is that queer old man?" I asked my husband.

"His name is Doong Lin Huo," he replied, "he has come to study the Gospel and is so grateful for what he is getting he has begged me let him do something to shew his gratitude."

Some days later one of the Evangelists came to me for some medicine for Mr. Doong, saying he was very ill with that foe of native and foreigner alike—dysentery. I had only one small bottle of expensive medicine which I kept for ourselves in case of emergency. It was unopened and when once opened I knew it would lose its strength. So I said:

"I have only medicine for ourselves."

"I fear if something is not done for Mr. Doong he will die," the Evangelist said as he turned away disappointed. This decided me and I hastily gave him out several doses. Later he came for more and a few days passed when Mr. Doong himself appeared dressed up in fine *borrowed* garments, and his face shining with the extra rubbing he had given it. Before we could prevent him he had prostrated himself before me knocking his head several times on the floor, saying, "Oh, lady, you have saved my life!"

The story of this man's conversion is of interest in that it is typical of thousands in China. His people were farming mountain villagers. Some years ago when visiting his village I was impressed with the picturesqueness of the situation, built as it is on the side of a steep mountain cliff above a rapidly running stream. As we went through this village street we walked up steps as if going up stairs.

Mr. Doong's family was large even for this land, it consisted of several of

37

the old passing generation, also his five sons and their wives and children and some of their sons' wives and their children. All lived within one enclosure. The family owned some land but as the mouths increased it was not sufficient for their needs and some sought employment, especially during the winter months. Mr. Doong himself was among these, he joined a low travelling theatrical company, as cook and lived as low a life while with them as any human being could well live. When the missionary first came across him he was using his animals during the slack winter months to escort travellers over the mountains west of his home.

One day the missionary arrived in the village with his party of preachers on their way to a famous goddess' temple situated two hundred Chinese miles further west among the mountains. Mr. Doong and his animals were hired for the journey. Day by day as the party stopped at noon and for the night preaching was carried on in the open. During those days Mr. Doong caught little else of the preaching than that they were speaking against the gods. He became alarmed and so sure was he that the great goddess would cause some terrible calamity to overtake them on their arrival at their destination he determined to leave the party as speedily as possible, and it was with a sense of real relief that he saw, as he thought, the last of them.

Some weeks later he had occasion to go to the distant city of Lin-Hsien far off among the mountains. Here he found the same missionary with his preachers still preaching as before—and no calamity had befallen them! He began to have doubts as to whether they might not be right after all. Every opportunity was taken advantage of to hear what they had to say with the result that when the time came for him to leave, he turned his face towards home a changed man.

His first step was to destroy the household gods, much to the horror and anger of his family and neighbors, who all believed him to have become bewitched by the foreigner and waited to see some dread judgment fall upon him. Surely facing such odds as bravely as this man did and with quiet steady calmness raises him to the place of a real hero.

His next step was to give up his opium. This he did without the aid of other drugs. He simply sought God's help and got it. His is one of the rare cases we have known of, where the terrible opium habit has been broken without human aid.

Then came his visit to our out-station to learn to read and understand the Bible. It was no easy task for either pupil or teacher at his age, but so earnest was he and diligent that in a few weeks he could read the Chinese

New Testament sufficiently well to get the meaning and in a few months had practically mastered its "characters."

Three years passed during which time Mr. Doong had won the highest opinions from missionaries and his fellow Christians. His name was suggested as a probationary evangelist, and although his lack of education was against him, his beautiful spirit, so gentle, and so full of love to all with whom he came in contact, seemed to more than make up for this lack and he was unanimously called to the preaching of the Gospel. As time passed, results from Mr. Doong's ministry amply justified this step, for wherever Mr. Doong was placed the work flourished and converts were added.

On one occasion the writer visited one of these places with her husband. It was a busy pottery centre, known far and wide for its unspeakable immorality. Yet even in this most difficult field Mr. Doong had gathered out a little company of believers.

I shall not soon forget the welcome we received on our arrival after a long trying dusty journey, at the door of the humble place where he lived and where we were to stay. He was so hearty and kind and yet had a certain dignity and courtesy which made me say inwardly, "Can this be the same man who was cook in a low theatrical company?" Yes he was the same, yet not the same, for his whole life, his looks, his wonderful power of holding heathen audiences for over an hour at a time all testified to the power of Christ to save and transform men.

At the close of our visit I told my cook to settle as was the custom with Mr. Doong for the coal we had used during the ten days we had been there. The cook returned to say Mr. Doong refused to take anything for it. I called the dear old man and protested that this would not do. He looked at me with tears in his eyes and said, "Mother, Shepherd, will you not allow me the privilege and pleasure of doing even this much for you, when you and your husband have done so much for me? What would I have been had you not come with this blessed Gospel?" With full heart and dim eyes I could only put my hands together and bow low my thanks.

When home on furlough I sent to a missionary for a photo of Mr. Doong for a lantern slide. In due course the photo arrived with a note from Mr. Doong himself, which ran as follows: "Dear Shepherd Mother, I thank you for the compliment you have paid me in asking for my photo. I would reciprocate and ask for yours but there is no need *for your countenance is engraved on my heart!*"

39

After an absence from our old field for some five years it was a great joy to both my husband and myself to have Mr. Doong once more our co-worker, but it was only for a brief period. Our hard pressed doctor needed the best man we could give him as Hospital Evangelist and Mr. Doong was chosen for this position. There he remained till advancing years with its increasing physical weakness forced his retirement and he returned home, but not to the home of the early years for now almost all had been won to Christianity, as well as many of his neighbors.

"For behold .... how that not many wise after the flesh, not many mighty, not many noble are called. But God hath chosen the foolish things of the world that he might put to shame them that are wise."

SKETCH IX

Heathenism As I Have Known It

Part 1—HEATHEN VERSUS CHRISTIAN WORSHIP.
Part 2—FACTS.

Heathenism As I Have Known It

"If thou forbear to deliver them that are drawn unto death, and those that are ready to be slain; if thou sayest, Behold we knew it not; doth not he that pondereth the heart consider it? And he that keepeth thy soul, doth not he know it? And shall not he render to every man according to his works?" (Prov. 24:11, 12.)

"If you can get our church people to really believe the heathen NEED the Gospel, you will have gone a long way to bring about the desired attitude towards Foreign Missions." So said a prominent Foreign Mission Secretary to the writer. Another Foreign Mission Secretary, who had spent many years on the Foreign Field as a missionary, suggested the subject for this Sketch, saying, "Draw it plain, for they need to know."

The subject is not a pleasant one; draw the picture of heathenism as you will, it can be only dark and repelling; neither *dare* one write all one knows....

1.—HEATHEN VERSUS CHRISTIAN WORSHIP.

Missionaries and converts were gathered in full force for their annual evangelistic campaign at one of the largest, most important centers of heathen worship in China—the Hsun-Hsien Fair or Festival. Inclement weather had somewhat delayed the influx of pilgrims. It was suggested that my husband and I take advantage of this fact to make a long planned visit to the temple of the goddess Lao Nai Nai, (Old Grandmother) who

40

drew to her shrine every year vast crowds of men and women of every class. (It is estimated that during the ten days of the winter festival alone, over a million pilgrims kneel before this image.)

We started quite early one morning hoping thereby to escape any possibility of great crowds. As we ascended the hill on which the temple stood, the road was lined on either side with booths and mat stalls where commodities such as pilgrims required, were sold. There were paper babies, made of brilliant colored paper on cornstalk frames. (The goddess was believed to have power to bestow living children in return for the paper offerings.) There were paper horses, and women and young girls, made to look very life-like, all of which were supposed to turn into the real kind for the use of the spirits beyond. Dice and gambling cards were much in evidence; also peep shows, which we were told were of the most obscene kind.

By the time we had reached the main entrance to the temple my courage had begun to fail, and gladly would I have backed out, but my husband felt we must go on. Passing through the great gates we entered a large court, on either side of which were crowds of men and women, some at tables, some seated on the ground, all feasting or gambling. In and out among these, peddlers passed calling loudly their wares. Utter confusion prevailed, but we had no difficulty in getting through to the court beyond; here, however, we found the crowd increasingly great. A large iron caldron resting on a pedestal stood in the center of the court surrounded by several men stripped to the waist, these were dancing and shouting as they stirred the fire in the caldron with iron sticks, the fire being fed by the paper offerings of the pilgrims. The men's faces and bodies were blackened by the paper ashes. The whole scene was most gruesome and reminded one of Dante's "Inferno."

The men, catching sight of us, demanded fiercely our paper offerings; one of them going so far as to seize me by the arm. I shrank in terror behind my husband, who urged me not to show fear, but to keep moving on; to go back now was impossible, for the whole crowd was moving on towards the right hand flight of steps leading up to the goddess' temple. On reaching these steps there was a pause and then a sudden rush, strain, and crush, when I found myself landed at the top of the steps, and my husband pushing me out of the crowd into a ledge of the balcony. Here we stood apart, almost hidden from the crowd.

What a sight the courts below presented! The crowds, seethed and

41

crushed; hundreds of explosives seemed to be fired every moment; the noise and confusion was indescribable. As we watched there were some things that made one's heart ache. Heathenism seemed stamped upon most of the faces. Old men and women could be seen helped along by younger ones. Some of these must have been well on to eighty; some were so frail and old as to be almost carried. We knew that these were old grandfathers or grandmothers being taken to the goddess' shrine to ask for a grandson.

As I turned from the sight, sick at heart, and closed my eyes for a moment, I seemed to forget my surroundings and before me rose a vivid scene in the dear homeland. I seemed to be once more in the old seat in Knox Church, Toronto. Our beloved, white-haired pastor, Dr. Parsons stood at the Communion Table. And I could hear him say, "That I might know Him, and the power of His resurrection, and the fellowship of His sufferings." The quietness, the reverential worship, the solemnity of the whole scene seemed as real as if I were there. But oh, the contrast as I opened my eyes on the scene before us! *That* was Christian—*this* heathen worship!

Taking advantage of a lull in the crowd, we entered the temple. On one side a group of Buddhist priests at a table were counting the money offerings. In the center was the shrine of the goddess, the image itself being far back almost out of sight. Immediately in front of the image a brass ring was suspended. A railing kept the pilgrims from getting too near, and as they knelt at this rail they threw their offerings through this ring. If the cash or coppers passed safely through the ring their petitions were sure to be granted! This, of course, encouraged many trys. It is said many millions of cash are thus offered year by year. The Buddhist priests use this money largely in gambling, drunkeness, and evil living.

We had seen enough. Gradually we made our way out by a back gate through the kindness of a friendly Chinese. We passed a small side shrine just behind the goddess' temple. Looking inside I noticed what seemed like a bundle of filthy rags, but seeing it move, I looked closer and found beneath a beggar—dying of starvation. From a near by eating house we procured a bowl of hot soup, but the poor creature was too far gone for help. There at the very foot of the heathen goddess the man died, with multitudes of her devotees passing him by without a thought of pity or sense of responsibility towards a fellow being. As soon as his last breath would be drawn, yes, and knowing what I do of heathenism, I dare say, even *before*, he would be taken out, thrown into a hole and barely covered;

while his poor beggar rags would be claimed by other beggars who perhaps before long, came to share the same fate. *That* is heathenism!

II.—FACTS.

"The tender mercies of the heathen are cruel."

Some years ago my husband and I went to a certain out-station where a camp of soldiers was stationed. A day or two before we arrived a man had killed one of the soldiers in a fight. The man escaped, but was later caught. (The utter injustice and often cruel oppression of the soldiers towards the people, lead us to believe quite possible, even probable, the man had right on his side.) He was taken before the military chief who said, "Since the man has killed one of yourselves you can do as you like with him."

For three days, while a platform was being erected, the poor creature was tortured by the soldiers with the most unspeakable refinement of cruelty. The platform on which he was to be executed was erected quite close to where we lived. The man was put on this high platform and in the presence of a great multitude of men, women, and children was cruelly done to death. We could hear the shouts of the people as they witnessed fresh signs of suffering. The awful details of this execution cannot be put on paper. That evening I called our chief Evangelist in and said, "Please write out as full a description of what has taken place as possible, for I wish to send it to the press with an appeal against such barbarism." And this was his reply,

"But what is the use, Teacher Mother? *This is not an isolated case.* It is done by the soldiers all over China, under like circumstances!"

Much more could be said on this phase of heathenism-cruelty. But we do not wish to dwell longer than necessary on any one part of this dark picture. But as I have studied the fruits of heathenism during these years of closest contact with a heathen people I have come to feel that this heartlessness and lack of pity is one of the most prominent features of heathenism.

One outstanding illustration of this. Li Shan Pao was the son of one of our Evangelists; he was a young lad of promise and we had been helping him through the High School at Wei Hwei Fu. One day he and some other lads were by the river near the school. Li Shan Pao undressed and went in for a swim, though the others tried to dissuade him, for the weather was still cold. He swam across the river and about half way back, when he

43

seemed to get into difficulties. The other lads on the shore called frantically to a passing boat for assistance. The men on this boat by just putting out an oar, or stretching out a helping hand, could have saved the boy, but though the lads on shore kept offering more and more money the only answer they received was, "It's not enough!" Then over the drowning boy they went without an effort to save him! When the missionaries came on the scene and drew the boy out, he was quite beyond help. *That is Heathenism.* But terrible as the guilt of these men may seem to us, yet are they not more guilty who deliberately close their eyes to their personal responsibility towards the dying souls of their fellowmen, whether at Home or on the Foreign Field?

The practice of Infanticide, which is one of the most terrible fruits of heathenism, is far more common than many believe. For several years I scarcely knew of its existence till my work began to take me out among the people. The three cases which I shall confine myself to in this Sketch, came to my notice within a short time of each other.

When preaching in a district among the hills Northwest of Changte, my husband, through what seemed a mere accident, found out that the custom existed through a wide region, of *putting all girls but one to death at birth in each family*! This they justified by saying the grain and water would not be sufficient for all if the population was not kept down!

A Chinese woman, belonging to a well-to-do family, called to see me one day. She had a beautiful baby boy in her arms. Her husband had just become a Christian and she seemed interested and some time later became one of our leading Christian women. But how dark her heart was then can be seen by what follows. A few weeks after her first visit she came again, but *without the baby.* The following conversation took place:

"Why! Where is your beautiful boy?"

"Oh, it's thrown away."

"But it was quite well when you came before. What disease did it have?"

"It did not have anything wrong." By this time I felt there must be something not right and determined to find out the truth. At last the woman told this story. One cold night the baby was lying on the outside of the "kang" or brick bed, it got out from under her cover and rolled off on to the floor. It was quite naked for the Chinese do not use night clothes, and instead of the mother taking the child up off the cold brick floor, she let it stay there all night. When she picked it up in the morning it was dead. I said, "Oh, how could you be so cruel?" She replied with a laugh, "I had plenty of other children and did not want the bother!"

When at an out-station a man brought a little baby, asking me to give it something to stop its crying as the mother was so tired of hearing it cry she did not want the child. I could not find anything the matter with the little one and told the father so. Some days later I saw the man in the yard and asked about the baby. He said it was "thrown away" meaning dead. I called my Bible woman and told her to find out the cause of the child's death. This is the story the father told her. On returning home the mother received her husband with angry looks saying, "I told you I don't want it; take it away." The father took the little one to a field away from the village and making a hole put the baby into it, but as he ran away the child's cries caused him to return and take it out again, but when the little one kept on crying he became impatient and throwing it back, covered it over and returned home. Who can say how many children meet a like fate in this heathen land every year?

What can one say of the injustice, cruelty, and oppression meted out to vast numbers of young brides and the younger wives and women by the older ones or their husbands? The marriage customs of China which demand that a young woman be under the care of, or rather guarded and watched, by her mother-in-law *is necessary so long as the morality of the men is what it is.*

My Bible woman and I were preaching in a heathen home. I had noticed a very fine young woman of about twenty among pur listeners. As we were preaching cries and sobs came from a room to the side of the court where we were. I signed to Mrs. Wang to find out the cause. A few moments later she called me out, and led me to the room from which the cries had come. As we passed through the court I noticed a poor idiot boy, a most pitiful sight. I found in the room we entered the fine young woman I had noticed among our listeners. She was sitting on the brick bed, a picture of utter despair. Tears were streaming down her cheeks, and as she rocked herself back and forth she moaned and sometimes cried aloud, always the same words,—"Oh, it is for life, for life!" I tried to discover the cause but failed. The only thing anyone would say was, "She often takes these turns." On our way home my women told me the truth. *This beautiful girl in the prime of life had been married to the idiot boy.* The boy's family needed a strong woman of ability to do their weaving and sewing. An extra gift to the Go-between on condition she secured such a wife for the idiot boy procured for them what they wanted. But what did they care for the broken heart? They were *heathen*!

The last phase of heathenism I will touch upon is—*Its utter hopelessness in face of Death.* Again and again have I asked heathen women what they had to look forward to after death; one and all have said, *only horror and fear.* Never has the story of my own dear Mother's wonderful death, passing as she did with the very Glory of heaven shining on her face, failed to move an audience of heathen women: again and again have they come to me at such times saying, "We want to know how to die like that. We suffer enough here, how can we go where there is no more suffering?"

Many dark scenes come to mind as I write; but what I have given is sufficient to justify us in saying that Heathenism is cruel; it is wicked, and heartless, and selfish, yes, and devilish!

* * *

"If THOU forbear to deliver them that are drawn unto DEATH ... He that keepeth THY SOUL doth not He know it!"

SKETCH X

The Blind Famine Refugee

The Blind Famine Refugee

The winter of —— was a sad, bitter one for those living in Eastern Shantung. The great Yellow River, truly called "China's Sorrow," had burst its banks, devastating a large area of thickly populated country. In spite of well organized famine relief administered by missionaries and other representatives of foreign countries (some of whom lost their lives from famine fever when engaged in this work), many people perished from starvation, fever or exposure.

Early one morning towards the end of February when the weather was still bitterly cold, a sad thing was happening inside a little wayside temple not far from one of the villages in this famine region. On the cold brick floor just in front of the idol's shrine lay a dying beggar. Famine was claiming one more victim. Beside him knelt his blind wife, swaying backwards and forwards moaning piteously. On the opposite side, nestling close to his dying father, as if for protection and warmth, slept a little boy of about six years of age.

All through that cold pitiless night the poor woman had knelt there listening to the hard breathing which told what she could not see,—that the end was near. As the day dawned the last struggle ceased. Quietly, with

46

the quietness and numbness of despair, the woman arose, felt for her child, awoke him, then grasping her stout beggar's stick with one hand and laying her other on the child's shoulder she motioned him to lead her away.

Reaching the road she hesitated. Where should they go to? Death from starvation seemed to await them on every side. As she stood there hesitating there came into her mind the remembrance of what someone had said long before—that a long way off, about one hundred miles distant, lived a man who could give sight to the blind. Quickly with a sense of desperation the poor blind beggar woman resolved to try to reach that man.

The sufferings of that journey can only be faintly imagined. They had no protection from the bitter winds by day, nor the cold frosty nights, but thin, torn, beggar garments. No resting place by day or night, but the roadside or the shelter of a wayside temple. Sometimes a whole day would pass when they failed to obtain even the few crumbs of black mouldy bread (made chiefly of chaff) usually thrown to them.

Later, when attempting to tell the story of these days, the poor woman seemed able to recall little else than the ever present dread she had, lest when they reach the doorway of the wonderful man who could give sight to the blind, it would perhaps be closed against them. Needless to say these fears were groundless, for when at last the mother and child reached the Mission gate almost dead from starvation and exhaustion, kind loving hands received them. They were taken into the Women's Hospital, cleansed, clothed, and fed.

The day following their arrival one of the missionaries went to Mrs. Ma, for such was the blind woman's name, and said:

"Mrs. Ma, I have been sent to tell you that the doctor has great hopes of restoring your sight. But you are far too weak for the operation yet. He says you are to have all the food you can eat, and that I am to get you anything you fancy. Now just tell me what you want."

At first the poor woman could not take it in. Then when Mrs. S——, repeated what she had said, and the meaning began to dawn upon her, she stretched out her hands and with an indescribably touching cry in her voice said, "If it is true indeed that I can really have what I most crave for, then oh, please just give me a little SALT!"

Reader, you, who have never known want, can scarcely comprehend the full significance of that request. "Just a little salt!" What deprivation, what agony of want is revealed in that word! To those of us who had seen something of the sufferings of famine victims, it meant volumes.

With tender loving care Mrs. Ma was nursed back to strength and health; but many weeks passed before the doctor pronounced her fit to stand the operation. Sight was restored to one eye, the other being quite beyond recovery. With glasses she was able to learn to read. The woman's gratitude knew no bounds. At first her eagerness to hear the Gospel and learn to read was largely due to this intense gratitude, but gradually the "True Light" entered her soul, and she became a sincere, earnest, humble Christian. Later she was appointed matron of the Women's Hospital where for twenty years she worked faithfully for the salvation of the women in the hospital.

Mrs. Ma's little son was put into the Boys' School soon after their arrival. As the years went by he passed through one Mission School into another, until he reached the Union Medical College of Peking. His whole life as a student had been such that the missionaries felt amply justified in paying his expenses through his medical course. He received his M.D., graduating with high honors in 19—. A large hospital had just been erected in an important city in North China. Dr. Ma was asked to become house physician of this hospital. Soon after his appointment to this position he married a fine Christian girl, one of the most promising graduates of the Women's College of Peking.

It was in Dr. and Mrs. Ma's cosy home near the hospital that the writer last saw old Mrs. Ma who was there on a visit to her son. She had long been too frail for active work. Her sight was gone, but the reflection of an inner light illumined her countenance as we recalled together the goodness of the Lord since the day she arrived at the Mission gate a poor starved Blind Beggar Refugee seeking Light.

SKETCH XI

Links in a Living Chain

Links in a Living Chain

A poor suffering woman lay in the ward of the Womens' Hospital at Changte. She had been there for over a month. Had she come earlier her life might have been saved, but ignorance and fear had kept her back till the terror of Death drove her to the Mission Hospital.

As the Missionary Doctor entered with her assistants the woman's face brightened up with a glad welcome smile.

"How much have you learnt to-day?" said the doctor bending over her kindly.

"Oh, doctor, I'm so stupid, and the pain is *so* bad I can't learn like the others. But oh, doctor, I have learnt this," and as she spoke she drew out from under the coverlet a sheet of paper on which was printed in large Chinese characters the hymn "Jesus Loves Me." And as she crooned over slowly the four verses making some slips the doctor listened patiently, correcting when needed. Then with a few tender words she passed on through the wards.

Not many days later, Mrs. Chang, the sick woman, had to be told nothing more could be done for her but she must return home to die. The long journey home over rough stony roads was borne with amazing fortitude, for had not her life been one long lesson in bearing hardness. For weeks she lay on the brick bed in her home at Linchang, a wonder to her family and neighbors. What was the secret of the change? She had left them with the horror and dread of death upon her face. She returned with her face shining with joy and openly stating she no longer feared death although she knew her days were few. She seemed happy and in peace. The hymn sheet was always in her hand and when asked why she was not afraid to die she would point silently to the second verse of the hymn and then chant aloud, trying to sing as she had heard others sing in the Hospital, but though the tune she sang could not have been recognized it sounded sweet in the ears of One who heard. Over and over that second verse was repeated for it contained that which was the Hope of her soul:

> "Jesus loves me, He who died,
> Heaven's gate to open wide,
> He will wash away my sin,
> Let His little child come in!"

Then the day came when according to Chinese custom neighbors and friends crowded into the chamber of death to see the end. As long as she had breath she urged her husband to go to the mission and learn the Gospel. She begged that none might go to her grave to weep, for she said, "I will not be there. I will be in Heaven." When the last moments came her face was illuminated with joy and she raised her hands as if to welcome someone as she passed away.

The effect of this deathbed scene was truly remarkable. Mr. Chang her husband, her only son and daughter and son's wife immediately became Christians. A quarrel which had separated Mr. Chang and his eldest brother for ten years was made up and this brother became an earnest Christian. Only a few months passed when a time of severe testing came to this family. The son's wife was taken ill and died. During her illness and at her death she witnessed as wonderful testimony to the Christian's hope as her mother-in-law.

The neighbors on the east side of the Chang's homestead were a large influential family named Fan. The younger Mrs. Chang's death-bed scene so touched one of the young men of this family that he determined to break away from the heathenism of his home and become a follower of Christ. His soul became so on fire for the Lord that he influenced many in his family until they were on the point of turning away from their heathenism. It was at this juncture that my husband and I began an aggressive evangelistic campaign in this town near their home, and great hopes were felt that the entire family would become Christian, when as in the case of Dr. Dwan (see "As Silver Is Refined") a series of events so terrorized the family that for over a year they refused to believe but that the gods were fighting against them for changing their belief. And is it any wonder? Almost immediately after young Mr. Fan became a Christian one calamity after another came upon the family till the climax was reached when one of the younger sons, about fourteen years old, went to visit a relative some ten miles distant. He never reached their home, but disappeared and was never heard of again. A little later another son who had become a seeker after Christ went to the Mission Hall apparently well was taken suddenly ill and before even a neighbor could be called passed away.

But in spite of these things, which to the heathen people of Linchang were certain proofs of the power of the gods to take revenge, young Mr. Fan stood true and within a year had won back several of his family. From this time the church grew in Linchang. Within a few years a nice Christian church and school house was erected by the Christians within sight of the Fans' home, the evangelist in charge also being supported by themselves.

Some years later it was the writer's privilege to assist her husband in a series of special meetings held in this little Linchang church, which during the ten days of the "Mission" was filled to its utmost capacity. Not soon could one forget the scenes of those days when one after another consecrated himself afresh to the Lord.

50

Two cases stand out prominently. One was that of a wealthy landowner who also was partner in a prominent business concern in Linchang. At considerable financial loss to himself he gave up this business to become a preacher of the Gospel. The second case was that of a proud Confucian scholar who at that time held a position of head teacher in a government school. He also caught the vision which forced him to resign his position in order to preach the Gospel.

Many times during those days as I witnessed the Holy Spirit working in the hearts of these men and women and saw signs of the light of the Gospel beginning to spread throughout that whole region I thought of that first little seed of truth sown in the heart of the poor suffering woman as she lay in the women's hospital in Changte.

SKETCH XII

Our First Woman Convert

Our First Woman Convert

A Mere Memory.

The following is but a brief memory of the long gone past. Even the name of the woman is forgotten but not the look on her pale patient face as she lay for weeks in the Mission Hospital—our first woman in-patient. Though almost thirty years have come and gone since those earliest days in North Honan the memory of this woman remains as one of the very few bright gleams in what was to us pioneer missionaries a time of darkness and peril.

The people were still bitter against us though a year had passed since a foothold had been gained in what we had so long looked forward to as our "Promised Land." Stories of the vilest nature widely circulated and believed did much to hinder the progress of the Gospel, and make the people fear and hate us. They believed we were capable of the very worst atrocities. Were I to attempt the plain record of many of these stories British law would forbid the publication.

It is little wonder, therefore, that our good doctor, a man of exceptional ability who had left brilliant prospects behind to come to China, chafed under the petty cases which came to the Hospital, and had more than once openly expressed his wish for some "good cases" which would help to open the people's hearts towards us. Before long his wish was abundantly gratified for three years later that hospital recorded *twenty-eight thousand*

51

treatments in one year, a goodly proportion being "good" cases.

The beginning of the breaking of the ice of prejudice came when one day a man wheeled into the hospital yard a barrow on which lay his sick wife. He seemed very loath to come but his poor wife appeared past feeling. It was most evident that only the hope of relief from otherwise certain death could have induced them to risk coming for help to the foreign doctor.

A little later the doctor announced a serious operation imperative. To this the woman gave her consent but the man hesitated. How impossible it is for those brought up in a Western land to form any conception of the struggle the man went through in face of such a sweeping away of life-long prejudices, but at last in face of that great enemy, Death, he yielded.

Oh, how we prayed for that case! There we were, a mere handful of missionaries in the midst of a bitterly hostile people many of whom were only waiting and watching for an excuse to attack and murder us. Should the operation prove fatal and the woman die under the doctor's knife it would have been quite sufficient to stir up a mob which would in all probability have destroyed us all. But the operation passed safely and during the weeks of convalescence the doctor's wife told into willing ears the message of a Saviour who died to "open Heaven's door." From the first the woman showed a wonderful keenness in learning the truth. While still unable to sit upright and scarcely strong enough to hold her book she studied almost constantly the simple Christian Catechism.

One day to my great surprise as I responded to a timid tap at my door, I found this dear woman shrinking and uncertain as to whether she would be admitted, and almost fainting from weakness. I led her gently in and as she lay on the sofa we talked together of the blessed Saviour. After all these years the joy I felt, in speaking of the precious truths to this first Christian Woman of North Honan, still remains. She seemed even then to have her thoughts turned toward Eternity for she loved to have me dwell on the Heavenly Home, and the hymn she loved best was:

"My home is in Heaven, my home is not here."

Soon her visits became quite regular and as she lay on the lounge listening and asking questions she was not the only one who was learning for many were the lessons she unconsciously taught me of fortitude under suffering, and the simpleness of childlike trust. It seemed at times as if every separate fruit of the Spirit in that glorious cluster could be seen in this

52

very babe in Christ. Love, joy, peace, long-suffering, gentleness, faith, meekness, all just shone from her countenance. One day shortly before her return home she asked a question concerning the Holy Spirit which showed what wonderful progress she had made in spiritual understanding.

Although she left us apparently cured, a few months saw her back again for treatment. It was then she was received as our first Probationer for Baptism but long before the year of probation had ended she had passed away in certain hope of entering into the Presence of her Saviour.

SKETCH XIII

Two "Rice" Christians

Part 1—THE "WOLF BOY."
Part 2—THE "WOLF BOY'S" MOTHER.

Two "Rice" Christians

Part I. THE "WOLF BOY."

As one travels Westward from the city of Changte, the country becomes more and more mountainous and rocky. Villages throughout that region are frequently troubled, during the cold winter season, by wolves, desperate with hunger venturing into the village streets injuring and sometimes carrying off children.

During the winter of —— a lad about fourteen years of age, named Cheng (surname) Woo-tse (given name), left his home near Changte to visit an aunt living in a village ten miles west of that city. One day, as the lad was going on a message, a great wolf rushed down the village street, and, before he could be driven away, jumped upon the boy clawing and eating part of his face.

For months the ignorant villagers did what they could to relieve the poor boy's terrible sufferings; but, alas, those who are at all acquainted with Chinese methods of treatment know how worse than useless such attempts would be. Only when it became apparent the boy would die were the people willing for him to be taken to the Mission Hospital.

Naturally this most unusual case aroused great interest; all came to know of the "Wolf Boy" as he was called. For almost a year he remained in hospital, carefully and tenderly nursed by his mother; her devotion to her boy being most noticeable.

The doctor and his assistants set themselves to do their utmost for what

53

they felt was one of the most difficult cases that had ever been in the hospital. The doctor sought to give the boy, as far as it was possible, a new face; but, after months of careful treatment and clever grafting, he was only partly successful. He succeeded in saving the sight of one eye and in forming practically a new mouth. But after the doctor had done all it was possible to do the boy still remained such a horrible sight he was forced to wear a mask.

While in the hospital all those months this poor torn lad won the hearts of all by his gratitude for every kindness, his cheerfulness and patience under great suffering, and his simple loving nature. The kindness shown them opened the hearts of both mother and son to the Gospel message and both became Christians. It was the boy, however, who received the story of the Saviour's Sacrifice with real joy. What it meant to him came out one evening at the weekly prayer-meeting.

The little group of Christians gathered were startled and deeply touched when the "Wolf Boy" suddenly began to pray; his face was so bound as to make speech difficult but this is what he said:

"O Lord! I thank Thee for letting the wolf eat my face, for if he had not I might never have heard of this wonderful Saviour."

When at last the time came for the boy and his mother to leave the hospital, the missionaries felt it would be heartless to turn the boy adrift to the "tender mercies of the heathen," so gave him the situation of water-carrier for their yard. Here he lived and worked amongst us for some years.

The writer can never forget this boy's sympathy and sorrow when one of the little foreign children, whom he looked upon as his friends, became sick unto death. Outside the sick child's door he waited and waited every moment he could spare from his work, hoping and praying for the word of hope that was not to come. When, at last, he was told the precious spirit was no longer with us, his grief was most touching.

Four years later the boy left us to take a situation at an adjoining mission station. Near this mission a river, wide and deep, flowed. It was here the wolf boy met his death. When bathing with some other lads he was carried out of his depth and drowned.

* * *

Many years have passed since this humble servant died, but there still

54

remains in many a heart a warm remembrance of the lad, so physically hampered, but through whom the Christ-life shone so brightly as to make him a blessing and an example to those who knew him.

Part II. THE "WOLF BOY'S" MOTHER.

"Faithful in that which is least."

The following brief sketch is a true and grateful tribute to the faithfulness of one who has been to the writer one of the greatest blessings a mother, with little children, could have—a faithful, devoted nurse.

As I write there comes before me a vivid picture of the scene in the hospital ward where I first saw Mrs. Cheng. On the wide brick platform or bed, which reached across one end of the room from wall to wall, were stretched a number of patients, each one on their own thin mattress or bedding, and each attended by their own friends; foreign nurses being unknown in China then. In the further corner of this "kang" or general bed, Mrs. Cheng bent over her poor mangled son, whose face was completely hidden by bandages.

On that first visit I remember being much impressed with the mother's soft voice and quiet dignified manner, and with her extreme gentleness in tending her child. Each subsequent visit increased the desire to secure this woman as a nurse for my children. Soon the opportunity came.

Mrs. Cheng soon found that months instead of days or weeks must elapse, before her child could leave the hospital. The question as to how she could support herself and her son while in the hospital became a serious one; she, therefore, gladly accepted my offer to meet their expenses in return for her help some hours each day with the children. By the time the doctor had pronounced the "Wolf Boy" ready to leave the hospital, Mrs. Cheng had proved herself such a blessing and "treasure" in our home that a warm welcome awaited her from the children as well as their mother and she was installed as their permanent nurse.

Less than one year after Mrs. Cheng came to us, that terrible cataclysm of horror—the Boxer uprising—took place, and we were all ordered to flee. With four small children the thought of that long cart journey *without Mrs. Cheng* was appalling; but would she come? Her boy still needed her to dress his face, and her old mother, of almost eighty, to whom she was greatly devoted, looked constantly to her for help. We laid our need before her and for one day she hesitated, going about the house as if dazed. At evening she came with tears, saying, "Shepherd Mother, I must go with you. My old mother weeps but tells me to go. My boy needs me, but he, too, says I must go, for the children need me most."

Days and weeks of terrible experiences followed, during which Mrs. Cheng proved herself a blessing to the sorely tried mother. Again and again she was tested as few have ever been; how she stood the tests we shall see.

The story of that journey has already been written, and only what specially concerns Mrs. Cheng will here be mentioned.

On the eleventh day of the journey a band of armed men came down upon our party like an avalanche, and in the melee Mrs. Cheng and our little daughter, Ruth, became separated from us. Can we ever forget, how, when men stood over the faithful nurse demanding the child, she refused to give her up, but lay upon the little one, and took blow after blow upon her own body? Only the greed for loot saved them, for the men seeing others getting our things left them to get their share.

That same night when again our party was facing what seemed almost certain massacre, several Chinese came to Mrs. Cheng urging her to leave us, promising to see that she would be taken safely back to her home if she would, but she refused.

About 2 o'clock that morning I heard the sound of weeping in the courtyard; going out I found Mrs. Cheng sitting by the steps weeping bitterly, and moaning aloud:

"I must go, I must go; they need me, even if they kill me I will go." Sitting down beside her we clung in our distress to each other. Then a strange thing happened. Two Chinese women came creeping towards us through the dark court, and kneeling down at our feet took our hands in theirs. Almost too surprised for words I said:

"Are you Christians?"

"We don't understand," they replied.

"Then why have you come to us now?"

"Because our hearts feel sorrow for you." These words but imperfectly convey the beautiful and touching sympathy of these heathen women, for as they spoke, tears were in their eyes, and their look and manner meant more than words. Before I had time to say more than a few words to them the call came to get into our carts.

Once, during the wonderful day of deliverances that followed, the cry was raised by the mob that surrounded our carts:

"Get the nurse out, drag her out, we will have her!" And for a few terrible moments it seemed we would lose her, but God in His great mercy heard the cry that went up for her. A man came through the crowd, evidently one of some influence, and shouted: "Don't touch her, leave her alone; don't you see there are children and they need her?" So we were allowed to pass on.

In those terrible days that followed, when almost starved, when sickness came to first one and then another, when all were exhausted and tried to the lost point of endurance, Mrs. Cheng thought not for one moment of herself, but only for those she served. During all those hard, hard days not a word of complaint or of her own sufferings escaped her.

Almost a month from the time we left our home we reached Shanghai and here we had to part with our faithful helper. It was arranged that Mrs. Cheng should go to a friend of ours in Chefoo till the troubles were over, and we return to the Homeland.

Last words of farewell were being said at Mrs. Cheng's cabin door, as her steamer was about to leave. The dear woman clung to me unwilling to part and her last words were:

"Oh, my Shepherd Mother, do take good care of the children!" So smiles were mixed with tears as we parted.

* * *

Two years passed. Conditions were once more becoming normal, or nearly so. Missionaries were returning to their various stations, but could we, who had been through that Baptism of Blood, ever be just the same as before? We had been spared for further service, while others had been TRANSLATED. Surely we had been saved to serve as never before. A new and difficult life was entered upon—the opening of new out-stations, the breaking of new ground. All through the years of that life when traveling constantly from place to place, Mrs. Cheng was a patient and willing sharer in all the hardness and a never failing source of comfort to me. Never once in all those years, that I can recall, did this woman ever get really angry or even out of temper with the children, and it was a life that tried temper and patience to the utmost.

The years have passed on and with them the *little* children from our care,

57

but Mrs. Cheng remains. Although sixty years of age she appears in some things to be renewing her youth! During the recent war, when we women were trying to do our "bit" through the Red Cross, Mrs. Cheng came to me one day and begged me to allow her to take my place at the sewing machine. At first I refused, but finally let her try but with some fear lest she break the needle. To my great surprise she was soon able to go on with the Red Cross work quite alone; indeed she came to make the soldiers' garments so well as to call forth special praise from the Red Cross Headquarters. This greatly surprised me, for I could never get her to attempt to learn the machine when the children were small. One day I asked her why this was so, and her reply was:

"*Then* I could not learn because the children filled my heart, *now*, my Shepherd Mother, it is empty!"

Let us take, in closing, a peep into Mrs. Cheng's own home. At break of dawn on New Year's morning, 1918, Mrs. Cheng, her only remaining son and his wife, and their three children, were busily engaged preparing their New Year's feast, which consisted of dozens (amounting probably to hundreds) of tiny meat dumplings, each one just large enough for one (?) luscious, mouthful. (These dumplings are to the Chinese at the New Year season what turkey and plum pudding are to the Westerner.)

When all was ready, even the pot or rather large caldron, at boiling point awaiting the precious dumplings, Mrs. Cheng gathered her household around her and together they knelt and worshipped the Christian's God. Heathen neighbors gathered about the open doorway and watched, in wondering but respectful silence, the kneeling group, and listened to their hymn of praise. Worship over, while the rest dropped dumplings into the bubbling water, Mrs. Cheng preached to the curious and questioning neighbors. Telling me of it afterwards she said,—"Of course, I could not preach, but I just told them what I knew of the Lord Jesus."

Oh, that all God's more favored children in every land would do just THAT.

SKETCH XIV

Daybreak in One Home

Daybreak in One Home

Part I. LITTLE SLAVE.

One of the most wonderful things about this wonderful old land of China, is the number, size and length of her great waterways. Millions of her people live, yes and die, on the large and small craft (chiefly the latter) which ply up and down these great streams.

Twenty-five days' hauling up one of these rivers from the Port of Tientsin, brings us to the town of Swinsen. There can be little doubt but that this place dates far back, for not far distant can be still seen the ruins of what was once—three thousand five hundred years ago, or before Moses led the Children of Israel out of Egypt,—the flourishing capitol of the Kingdom of China.

The Wang family, for many generations, had made their home in this curious old town of Swinsen. To trace the history of one section of this family, as I think you would like to hear it, we shall have to go back forty years. Could we about that time, have taken a peep through one of the gateways on a narrow street of this town, we would have seen a strange sight.

Standing in the centre of the court, and surrounded by a rough mocking group, was a young girl. She was dressed in all the gaudy garments of an Eastern Bride, but her finery served only to show forth the more conspicuously how ungenerous Nature had been in the matter of good looks. Tall and very thin, with a slouchy uncertain manner which gave her loose ill-fitting garments the appearance of being made for another, and with deep smallpox marks covering her face, and only partially concealed by powder and paint, she certainly did not appear the beautiful bride they had been led to expect.

A storm of ridicule and scorn was kept up by the group surrounding her. "Evidently," said one, "she has been brought up in a poorly-managed home or why have her feet been allowed to grow so large?"

59

"Were we not promised a beautiful, rich, clever, bride, with tiny feet?" said another. And the storm of abuse upon the innocent girl and absent "go-between" became so bitter as to make the poor creature shrink in terror. At last, like an animal brought to bay, she turned pleadingly towards a bright young man standing on the outskirts of the group, her bridegroom of a day, who till that moment seemed heartily to enjoy the fun of tormenting her. Catching her pleading terrified look he flushed as if with shame; then calling out sharply,—"Enough, enough! Let her alone. She is not to blame, and, anyway, she is here to stay." With this he gave her a not ungentle push towards the door of their apartment, then hastened through the gate and disappeared down the street.

As is the custom in China the Wang household was ruled with a rod of iron by the old grandmother. And the old lady certainly had her hands full for there were four sons, and four daughters-in-law, also numerous grandchildren. The new daughter-in-law was no favorite with her, and young Mrs. Wang, as we shall call her, had a hard and bitter life. All the women of the family joined in making her the drudge. One would have to understand heathenism and the conditions of a heathen home to fully comprehend what refinement of cruelty and meanness can be exercised by women under like circumstances. Again and again Mrs. Wang was tempted, as she knew so many other brides had been, to end her wretchedness by jumping down the well or taking opium poison, but something seemed to keep her from this awful deed.

One day there arrived to comfort the poor girl's heart a tiny stranger. Because it was a girl the other members of the family took no interest in its arrival, but the mother's heart, crushed and starved for so long, went out to her little daughter. She thought long for a beautiful name for her, and at last decided to call her "Lily Blossom." But when the old grandmother heard of her choice of a name she was furious, and asserted her authority in no uncertain manner, declaring, "No girl in my family will ever receive such a name. Why! it is just tempting the fairies to send us *only girls*. Her name is to be SLAVE." And Slave she was called.

The child grew up pretty and attractive, surprisingly so considering the coarse and unattractive surroundings in which she lived. She was her mother's constant companion, and even when very young would try to shield her mother from the blows often showered upon her.

When Slave reached her sixth birthday preparations were made to have her feet bound. Three or four women were needed for the performance. One to hold the child, a second to bandage, and one or two more to pull the bandages. A veil must be drawn over one terrible hour. Then we see her rolling from side to side on the large brick bed in a state of semi-consciousness. Her shrieks and cries had become reduced to low moans.

At last her mother in pity offered to loosen the bandages, but little Slave pushed her away with all her remaining strength, saying, "No, no, I want my feet small, I must have my feet small." And the mother knowing well the bitterness and cruelty she had suffered because of her own feet being allowed to grow to almost natural size, yielded.

For months Slave was practically a cripple, then gradually she learned to balance herself on her crushed and broken stumps of feet. Later the child's delight knew no bounds, for everywhere she went her tiny feet, clothed in beautiful embroidered shoes, attracted the admiration of all.

* * *

Seven years have passed and we now find Slave a beautiful girl of thirteen. Her beauty had been much talked of, and great expectations were indulged in regarding her marriage. The child outwardly seemed to take more interest in making her pretty shoes than in these discussions regarding her future "Mother-in-law's home," but in reality she was a keen and interested listener to all that was said on the subject.

More than one "go-between" had visited the home for the purpose of arranging a match with Slave, but the family knew her market value and were hard to please. At last a woman came from whom Slave instinctively shrank. Yet it was she who succeeded in satisfying the demands of the family. This woman stated positively that the "Mother-in-law's home," for whom she was the middle-woman, was all that could be desired. They owned considerable property, and were the chief family of their village. As to the man himself, why he was all a girl could wish for or be proud to call a husband,—young, handsome, clever, and so on.

The outcome of it all was the usual gifts were exchanged and Slave's fate was sealed for life.

Two short years passed then word was received from Slave's mother-in-law's home that the wedding must take place on a certain date in the near future. During the busy days of preparation that followed, Slave's heart palpitated many times as with mixed feelings she thought of the future. Then alas, all too soon the eventful day arrived, when two Sedan chairs were set down at the Wang's gateway. The one containing the waiting bridegroom, was handsomely decorated in blue and silver, but the bride's chair was even more gorgeous in its trappings of gold and crimson.

When the time came for farewell, tears of real sorrow were shed, but little Slave's heart was too full of the handsome young bridegroom to permit such sad feelings remaining long. No sooner was she safely behind the curtains of her chair than she arranged with utmost care, her veil and ornaments, seeking meanwhile to get a glimpse of the one who was to be hers for life. Often had she pictured to herself the "handsome young man" described by the "go-between," and it was with only joyous anticipation that she thought of the future. No response, however, came from the other chair.

The journey was soon over, and as they approached her future home Slave became increasingly nervous and shy. She could easily have caught a glimpse of her bridegroom's face through her veil as they alighted from their chairs, but her eyes seemed glued to the ground. She felt herself led through the crowd of noisy spectators, and was conscious that he was beside her. Together, side by side, they knelt before the household gods. But it was not till she had been led to the bridal chamber and seated on the brick platform or bed, with her garments arranged to the best advantage, that the crowd was admitted and her veil was raised.

A low murmur arose at the sight of her great beauty. Still little Slave's eyes would not rise. It was not till all had left and she was alone with her husband that her eyes rose with one swift glance. But, alas, poor child, it was not to see the bridegroom of her dreams, but instead she saw a man old enough to be her father,—a man with the marks of a debauched and wicked life plainly written on his countenance,—a typical opium slave; in other words a man only in name, rather a brute in human form!

As Slave caught sight of this man standing there, intoxicated with wine, and looking like a beast about to pounce upon its prey, the shock of disappointment was too great. Her face became deathly white, and with a piercing cry,—"My mother, oh my mother," she fell forward unconscious.

We must leave our little friend to enter the darkness alone, only one of multitudes in this dark heathen land of China whose innocence and happiness are year by year sacrificed to the greed of gain and cruel marriage customs of their own land.

We shall see later how the Light that can lighten the deepest darkness, came at last into little Slave's life, giving peace and hope.

Part II. SLAVE'S FATHER.

Slave was gone! As really lost to her parents as if she were dead. When the truth concerning the man she now belonged to for life became known, her mother wept long and bitterly, but there was no redress; they had to bear as others had borne, who had been deceived by an unprincipled "go-between."

Some months after Slave's marriage, there came to fill her place two fine twin boys. Mrs. Wang's day had dawned at last. The old grandmother could not do enough for her and the once despised and ill-treated drudge was waited on hand and foot by the other women, at the command of the old lady.

For three whole years this state of things lasted, then one day the grandmother announced her intention of *making the two boys take the smallpox*. (Many of the Chinese believed that children must have the smallpox when young or they will not grow up strong). The mother's heart sank as she thought of what the result *might* be. She ventured to protest but was silenced by a shower of blows. The grandmother took both of the fine healthy boys to a neighbor's house where they had smallpox, and kept them there a whole day to ensure them getting the disease. A week later both became ill.

We must draw a veil over the horror of the days that followed the agony of the mother, the despair of the father, the rage of the grandmother when she saw the children would die, and the ill-concealed malice of the other women. A few days passed when a little body, wrapped in a piece of old matting, was carried by the father to the children's pit outside the city. A little later this scene was repeated, and Mrs. Wang's day of happiness ended.

The cruel death of their two beautiful boys was the beginning of dark days for *our* Mr. and Mrs. Wang. The old grandmother died shortly after from excess of rage. (The fits of rage to which women give way in China cannot easily be understood by the Westerner). It was in one of these attacks, caused no doubt by disappointment at the result of her treatment of her grandchildren, that the poor old autocrat collapsed and died. The day before the funeral was to take place the old husband was found dead in bed.

An expensive funeral and excessive feasting which followed and which custom required reduced the family to desperate financial straits.

63

The days following the funeral were tempestuous ones for the Wang household, and the "domestic typhoons," as they have been correctly described, were fiercer and more frequent than ever. At last the day came when the family mutually decided to separate, which they did in true Chinese fashion—each couple would be responsible for their own finances, but would continue to live as before "within the one gate."

This arrangement would have been favorable to our branch of the family had not Mr. Wang lost his situation as teacher almost immediately after the change. Then followed several moons (months) of fruitless search for employment. Everything that could be was sold or pawned to get food.

One day Mr. Wang's boatman brother returned from the coast. He told them of a man who had come up on their boat who was looking for a teacher for a missionary living in an adjoining province, and he urged Mr. Wang to take this position. The women-folk, however, bitterly opposed saying, "If he once gets under the spell of the foreigner we shall never hear of him again." But they could not starve, and when it was learned the salary would be considerably more than what he had been getting even the women yielded.

Mr. Wang was himself only half inclined to go, for he could not get out of his mind the remembrance of stories he had heard of wholesale poisoning carried on by the missionaries.

Shortly after his departure a little girl came to comfort Mrs. Wang in her loneliness. Now that she was her own mistress, she chose a pretty name for the child, little dreaming what a beautiful herald it was of the brighter day so soon to dawn, she called it Spring!

One morning when little Spring was just three weeks old, the Wang family received a great surprise. They were all seated at their own doorsteps or squatting around the court, each with a bowl of millet poised in one hand and a pair of chop sticks in the other, when the front gate opened and who should appear but Mr. Wang. It was as if a bomb had fallen! In a few moments the court was crowded with curious neighbors, all eager to hear the reason for his return.

The truth in brief was that he had reached the Mission Compound safely, had been well received by the other Chinese teachers, had been in the missionary's home and had taught him and his wife for one day, but that night had been seized with sudden panic lest he get under the spell of the missionaries, and had gathered up his belongings and when all were asleep had quietly slipped away. This, however, was not just how Mr. Wang told it to the waiting crowd. He found it necessary to add a good many embellishments to make it a less humiliating story than it would otherwise have been, and these additions were not always favorable to the foreigners.

The family had to face the fact that there were three "mouths to fill" and some work must be got, but weeks of searching resulted as before in failure. Our friends would certainly have starved had not other members of the family given, sometimes almost thrown, food to them. At last in sheer despair Mr. Wang accepted a position in the Yamen (City Hall) for just his food. Thus Mrs. Wang was left to battle with her little babe alone. The cold pitiless winter faced her and bitter indeed did she find the struggle for existence. To earn even three and a half cents a day, she was obliged to sit at her spinning wheel far into the night, with her babe inside her wadded garment to keep it warm.

* * *

During those long winter months Mr. Wang sat at his desk in the Yamen the face of the missionary seemed to come before him vividly—so kind, so true, so different from any face he had ever seen before.

Gradually he came to the point of resolving that had he another chance he would return to the missionary. The opportunity was nearer than he imagined.

While at his work one morning he heard an unusual commotion outside. Stepping to the front gate he found a great crowd hurrying towards the river. A man shouted to him, "Two foreign demons are coming up the river. Come and see the fun."

Without so much as a thought for his work awaiting him, Mr. Wang caught up his teacher's long gown to accelerate speed, and before the man ceased speaking had started to run with the others. His behaviour on this occasion at least was quite unworthy of a proud Confucian scholar, all of whom pride themselves on imitating the sage in never making haste under any circumstances.

Just as the tiny house boat, with two foreign men standing on its deck, came in sight, Mr. Wang reached the river bank. Had he tried he would have found it difficult to say why he trembled so. He was only conscious of an intense desire that one of these men might be *his* foreigner. At last as he recognized the missionary he had taught for a day, he could scarcely repress a cry of joy, or wait till the boat was drawn up to where he stood.

65

Then, not waiting for the plank to be put down, he leaped on board and faced the astonished missionary, who looked his amazement as he recognized him.

Before the other could find words, Mr. Wang, making a low bow hurriedly asked forgiveness in a few humble words. He ended by saying, "I know, sir, you are not what people say you are. I was wrong, forgive me. If you will take me back I will be glad to teach you."

While he was speaking the missionary's face was a study—surprise, annoyance, relief, pleasure—all came in turn. The missionary, who could now speak the Chinese language a little, laid Ids hand kindly on the young man's shoulder and said:

"Not a word more, Mr. Wang. I am in need of a teacher so you may consider yourself engaged, but you must be ready to start back with us three days from now."

The poor fellow looked his gratitude but could find no words. As he turned to leave the missionary called him back and said in a low voice as he handed him some money, "Take this, you have a wife and she must be provided for, we will reckon later." This thoughtful act completed the capture of Mr. Wang's heart. From that moment he became the devoted follower of the missionary although as yet he knew nothing of his message.

Three days later found Mr. Wang settled in his little "tsang" or cabin on the missionary's houseboat. Next to his was the larger cabin occupied by the two missionaries as sleeping and living apartment. A partition of open woodwork covered with paper separated the two cabins. Mr. Wang had not been in his compartment very long before he had, in true Chinese fashion, by moistening the tip of his finger and applying it to the paper partition, made a hole sufficiently large to enable him to watch all that passed in the adjoining cabin without himself being seen. Day by day he spent every moment he could get at his self made vantage ground. How those men puzzled him! As he noticed how quiet and orderly, and above all how strangely happy they were, without being boisterous, he became conscious of a growing sense of respect and admiration. Before they had reached their destination, the missionary's home, Mr. Wang had lost every trace of doubt or fear of the foreigners.

Mr. ———, the missionary, was a keen judge of character. His knowledge of human nature was gained in the slums of a so-called Christian city, and it was well for him that such experience had been gained before meeting the more complex problems of the Chinese character. As day by day the missionary studied with Mr. Wang he became more and more convinced that this man must meet Christ first in him, His representative, for he found him sharp, keen, critical, and alas, utterly untrustworthy. But the day came when Mr. Wang testified, when he was being received into the Church, "I learned first to love the Pastor, then to love his Saviour."

Part III—SLAVE'S RELEASE.

Six years have passed since Mr. Wang entered on his duties as teacher to the missionary. During all those years he had been an invaluable assistant to Mr. —— in the strenuous and difficult work of opening a new mission station at the large and important city of C——. The time had now come when it was thought best for Mr. Wang to bring his wife from their old home. A small cottage was secured just opposite the mission gate for them, and here a happier life began for Mrs. Wang than she had ever thought possible.

Mr. Wang, like so many Chinese Christian men, thought his wife too stupid to learn, and when she first came in touch with Mrs. ——, the missionary's wife, she was practically a heathen. As she came in with little Spring, now a bright little girl of nearly seven, the foreign woman could scarcely hide her disappointment when she saw Mrs. Wang, she was so extremely (shall I use the word) *ugly*, so untidy, slouchy, and even far from clean. Yet there was a look in those small deep set eyes which said plainly, "Yes, I know how different I am from you, but oh, I do want you to love me." And the other felt herself strangely drawn to her. Before long a deep and abiding affection sprang up between the two, so different, yet at heart one.

Many times in the lesson periods that followed Mrs. —— was tempted to give up in despair, Mrs. Wang was so slow to learn. One day after a particularly discouraging time of study, Mrs. Wang turned to her teacher and said, "Teacher Mother, do not be discouraged because my mind is like a sieve, for my heart has Jesus there."

The evidence of the new life within soon began to be seen in the changed, happier, more restful face, and in the cleaner, tidier garments. Willingly she allowed little Spring's feet to remain unbound, which meant much at that time when women and girls with unbound feet were unknown.

Although Spring had not the beauty of her older sister, Slave, she was bright, quick, in her ways like her father, and most affectionate. From the first contact with the missionaries the child's heart seemed open to the Gospel, she came soon to show a love for the Saviour unusual in one so young. The greatest treat little Spring could have in those early days was to be allowed to play with the gentle fair-haired foreign child of her own age.

One day the two children wandered outside the backgate into the fields beyond. Suddenly they came upon some dogs devouring the body of a little child. Spring, to whom such a scene was not unknown, looked on unmoved, but the tenderly guarded foreign child gazed in speechless horror, then screaming loudly ran towards home. Her mother, anxious at her disappearance, had just reached the gate when the child appeared almost frantic with terror and shock. A word was sufficient for the mother to learn the cause of the trouble. "Oh, Mother!" cried the child, sobbing on her mother's breast, "I see it now, a dear little baby. Oh, mother, mother, those terrible dogs. I can never forget it."

That night the mother knelt long beside her child's bedside. Other little ones had come and gone. This child seemed like a delicate lily, too sensitive and high strung for such a land as China, where outside the Mission Compound one could never tell when one would come upon a scene that might hurt and shock.

Some time later the child was taken ill. There was no doctor near and once more the parents went down into the Valley of the shadow of death with a precious child. Meningitis developed. Spring and her mother watched and waited outside the child's sick door for some word of hope. But after days of great suffering the little one was taken to where there will be "no more pain, neither sorrow nor crying."

A day later missionaries and Christians gathered about the open grave beside which rested the little coffin almost covered with beautiful flowers. It was then that Mrs. Wang recalled the cruel death of her two boys and what had been done with their little bodies. The contrast was indeed great: here were every token of love and honor for the precious remains; but what moved Mrs. Wang end went to her heart was the look of Hope written on the mother's face as they all sang together—

> "Little children, little children.
> Who love their Redeemer
> Are the jewels, precious jewels,
> His loved and His own.
> "Like the stars of the morning

His bright crown adorning,
They shall shine in His beauty
His loved and His own."

As these words sank deep into Mrs. Wang's very soul, there came a great yearning that her own people might hear of this Gospel that gives a soul a hope after death.

* * *

Sometime after her little friend's death, Spring entered the mission school for girls, the first girls' school to be opened in that part of China. Year by year as they passed, Spring grew in the love and esteem of her teachers. Her bright, happy ways and true Christian character endeared her to all. But the one Spring loved most of all was the mother of the friend she never forgot. On one occasion when the writer was home on furlough, she received the following letter from Spring: "Dear Teacher Mother, Come back very soon. As one who is hungry longs for food and one who is thirsty for drink, so my heart longs for you!"

When fifteen years of age Spring graduated with such distinction that she was sent to the advanced school for girls in Peking. Upon her return she became assistant teacher in the Mission Girls' School.

About this time Mrs. Wang's health broke down. A little daughter had come whom they named "Brightness." Through all the months of weakness and failing health, the poor suffering woman showed forth a true spirit of patience and resignation. One day an urgent call came for the missionary's wife to go and see the sick woman. Hastening to the little cottage across the way, she found the court empty so entered the door unannounced, and passing through the outer room she lifted the curtain that served for door into the room where she could see dimly the form of her loved friend lying on the brick bed.

There was no mistaking the look which plainly told the last call had come to Mrs. Wang. Overcome with the shock of seeing the end so near, Mrs. —— sank down beside her friend and wept bitterly. Slowly the dying woman raised her hand and stroked the head of the weeping woman, and with difficulty said, "Don't grieve for me. There is much I want to say, but the time is too short. Listen! My child, my little Slave, does not know about the Saviour. Help Spring to go to her before it is too late."

There was a long silence broken only by suppressed weeping from Spring

69

who was standing by. Then Mrs. Wang continued, "And you, my friend; thank you again for bringing this precious Saviour to even me. And you have helped me so much."

"No, no," said Mrs. —— unable to keep silence longer. "It is you who have helped me. Your patience under trial has been a constant rebuke to me for my impatience." She could say no more for even while she was speaking the Glory of the unseen world seemed to shine on the dying woman's face.

* * *

Some months after her mother's death the way was opened for Spring to visit her father's old home. She had many times longed and prayed that she might fulfil her mother's dying request. With some difficulties Spring found where her sister lived and as she drew near the house her heart rose in earnest prayer for her sister's conversion.

An old woman responded to her knock at the gate, to whom Spring made herself known, then asked to see her sister. The old woman who turned out to be Slave's mother-in-law, directed her to the door of the room where we last parted with poor Slave—a broken-hearted bride.

Tapping gently on the door and receiving no answer, Spring entered. On the long brick bed at one end of the room lay her sister. The wasted frame and racking cough told all too plainly Slave's days on earth were few. As Spring stood looking at her sister for a moment, almost too overcome to speak, she thought of her mother's words, "before it is too late."

For three days Spring remained with her sister. Fortunately for them both Slave's husband was not at home, and the old mother-in-law left them alone only too glad to have someone to relieve her from waiting on the sick one.

When Spring described to her sister their mother's beautiful death, tears ran down Slave's cheeks as she said, "Oh, that I too could have such a hope!"

"You can, my sister," eagerly cried Spring. "I have come as mother wished, to tell you how you can go to where she is." Then patiently and lovingly she opened up to her sister, step by step, the glorious Gospel of a Saviour from sin and a hope after death. Slave listened and drank in the message as one parched with thirst would drink from a living spring.

Once when the sisters were talking closely together, Slave suddenly broke

70

into a passion of uncontrollable weeping. Then came little by little as she had strength to tell it, the story of those terrible years since she left her father's home. At last as if words failed her, she loosened her garment and revealed her shoulders and back covered with bruises and healed scars, silent witnesses to the cruelty of the past.

Gradually the Peace and Hope born of her new found faith came into Slave's poor starved soul. And as the sisters parted never as they knew well to meet again on earth, Slave said, "Yes, it is different now, I shall be in heaven before you. I have no more fear now. But pray for my husband."

* * *

> There is a Love that longs with deep affection
> To gather all the sinsick sons of men
> Beneath its wings of shelter and protection,
> And give them health again.
> It is the love of Jesus, sweet with longing,
> His full salvation to the world to give,
> Crying to all the dead, earth's highways thronging,
> "Come unto Me, come unto Me, and live."
> *By Annie Johnson Flint.*

Made in the USA
Lexington, KY
17 April 2014